Seeing the In
Ordinary people of
extraordinary faith

Faith Cook

EP Books (Evangelical Press): Unit C, Tomlinson Road, Leyland, PR25 2DY

epbooks@10ofthose.com

www.epbooks.org

This edition 2017

British Library Cataloguing in Publication Data available

ISBN 978-0-85234-407-1

To my sons,

Jerry, Oliver, Simon and Edward

Contents

Foreword

As a young teenager, from a non-Christian background, the first Christian book I read was a short biography of Hudson Taylor. It made a profound impression upon me. A few years later, while doing National Service in Germany, I read the larger two-volume biography of Hudson Taylor. As I write, I have taken the second volume from my bookshelves. It has fallen open at a page where I wrote in pencil on 8 August 1951, aged twenty, 'What a blessing these words have been to my soul. Especially the words "to know Him" and "to make much of the Lord Jesus."' I remember still how God used the correspondence Hudson Taylor had with a friend to speak to my spiritual need at the time. Faith Cook's book has prompted me to thank God for the place Christian biographies have had in my spiritual pilgrimage. It has also reminded me of the unique benefit they should continue to be, and the importance of recommending them to others.

Christian believers should never be in doubt about the value of biography. The Bible gives an important place to the record of God's dealings with believing men and women. No chapter is a greater inspiration to faith than Hebrews 11. It draws attention to the experience of God's people over many generations, and carefully points out the lessons we may learn from their lives.

The spiritual 'income' or 'revenues' from reading the ten brief biographies in this book are considerable. First, they honour God. In the account of each person's life we see how God chooses ordinary men and women like ourselves to be united to his Son, and to serve him. The Christians whose stories are told here would have confessed that they were 'jars of clay' to whom God entrusted the treasure of the glorious gospel of his Son to show that the power is his and not ours.

Second, they illustrate the important contribution of Christian women, and Christian wives in particular. I went recently to a prominent contemporary biographer's lecture on the writing of secular biography. All of his biographies so far have been of men. In the question time that followed his address, he was asked whether he would write the biography of a woman. His answer was that he saw no reason at all why he should not. Significantly, he then carefully made the point that in each of his biographies he had had to cross the gender line because women held a strategic place in the life of each of his subjects. Faith Cook's book demonstrates the key role of wives like Elizabeth Bunyan, Harriet Newell and Martha Nelson, and women like Lavinia Bartlett, of whom Charles Spurgeon said, 'My best deacon is a woman.'

Third, they encourage and inspire. None of these personalities is a well-known name in Christian history. Some of them lived in the shadow of famous Christians. Their lives, however, were equally important, and perhaps in God's estimation particularly so. It is not for us to evaluate our contribution to the body of Christ, but rather, like these men and women, we are to be faithful to the unique opportunities God gives us. My hope and prayer are that God may graciously use the inspiration of these ten lives to prompt us to read more Christian biographies. As we take a good look at the example of godly men and women, may their faithfulness instruct and inspire us.

Derek Prime

William Darney: 'Scotch Will', pedlar and preacher

William Darney, a Scotsman, was born around 1710, and became one of the earliest itinerant preachers of the eighteenth-century evangelical revival. A pedlar and shoemaker by trade, he combined his daily work with his preaching. Beginning in 1741 in the Rossendale area of Lancashire, he continued to preach for almost forty years, mostly in the north of England.

The people listened intently as the old Scottish preacher, his long white hair flowing to his shoulders, urged his congregation to remain steadfast in the faith, no matter how severe the sufferings they must endure. 'Take courage!' he exhorted. 'Christ will soon return "in flaming fire, taking vengeance on them that know not God."'

At that very moment the clamour of an approaching mob drowned the preacher's voice. In rushed the deputy constable of Almondbury, holding his baton aloft and closely followed by an enraged crowd. 'I charge you,' cried the constable, 'in the name of King George, to come down.'

'I charge you, in the name of the King of kings, that you let me go on with my sermon,' was William Darney's swift reply.

'Pull him down,' commanded the constable to his waiting henchmen.

Glad of an opportunity to demonstrate their hatred of the new preaching which was having so powerful an effect on the people of Almondbury, near Huddersfield, the mob seized Darney by his long white hair and soon dragged the old preacher to the ground.

Although his friends struggled to save him from their hands, they were outnumbered and before long the crowd had hauled him into the street and were kicking him mercilessly with their iron-clad boots. Frog-marching the injured man to the vicarage, where they knew the vicar would readily lend his support to such barbarity, the crowd then threw him to the ground once more until it was feared his injuries might prove fatal. Only then did Darney's friends manage to rescue him from his tormentors and escort him to safety.

William Darney was no stranger to such maltreatment. For thirty years it had been his constant lot as he brought the message of the judgement and mercy of God to the people in the evangelical revival of the eighteenth century. 'Scotch Will,' as he was commonly known, had probably been converted in the revivals in Scotland between 1733 and 1740 under the preaching of James Robe of Kilsyth. Possibly Robe never knew of the work of God in the young man's soul, for by 1741 he had left his home country and had travelled south as far as Lancashire.

A pedlar by trade, Darney began hawking his wares from village to village, selling haberdashery and mending shoes. Advertising his goods, he would gather a crowd, but always with a dual purpose, for the passion of his life was to preach to the people, spreading the knowledge of the righteous anger of God against sin and the hope of forgiveness through Christ. A man of immense physique with a broad Scottish accent, Darney could not fail to have a traumatic effect on the people who lingered to hear him. His burning zeal and passionate denunciations of sin stirred up powerful reactions amongst them: many were converted to God, while many others were incited to fury.

The Rossendale area of Lancashire, like most other parts of Lancashire and Yorkshire, had known little gospel light in the past. But William Darney's forthright preaching heralded the breaking of a new day of God's grace for the north of England. At Heap Barn, a hamlet near Bacup, in Lancashire, the response to his preaching was typical of the reaction he evoked wherever he went. Each day for two weeks peasants, farmers and pack-horse drivers gathered to hear the message he preached, and there a group of young men were powerfully affected by his words and some were converted.

Opposition flared up as well. A woman, whose impressive size and ferocious looks could hardly fail to demand attention, lifted high her dung-fork and threatened to knock the preacher over unless he desisted from preaching immediately. Undeterred by her threats, Darney calmly continued his sermon, and when a young man named John Madin came to tell him of the work of God in his soul, Darney hugged him enthusiastically, exclaiming, 'You are the first-fruits of my labour in this place!'

Often Darney would conclude his services by teaching the people to sing verses he had composed which rendered his message into song. Doggerel poetry it might have been, and crude to a refined ear, but it was an effective means of retaining his words in the minds of the people.

As news spread from one community to the next of the pedlar-preacher whose sermons could both terrify and console his hearers, the people gathered in even greater numbers.

Nor was it adults alone who were affected. One small boy living near Rochdale was given the irksome task of rocking the baby's cradle so that his mother could be free to listen as Darney preached in an adjacent room. Ingeniously, however, the lad devised a means of tying a string to the cradle and then creeping to the edge of the crowd. Now he could both rock the cradle and hear the preacher at the same time. In later years he dated his conversion from the words he heard that night.

As converts multiplied Darney, whose livelihood depended on travelling from place to place, would band them together into small societies which could meet regularly for mutual fellowship in his absence. Whenever he himself returned to the area he would then minister to these scattered groups of believers.

Gradually Darney began moving further east into Yorkshire, selling his wares and preaching, until by the summer of 1744 he was on the outskirts of Haworth. William Grimshaw, curate of

Haworth, was not pleased. Only recently converted himself, Grimshaw feared Darney might be preaching another gospel which would undermine his own preaching. So he determined to attend one of Scotch Will's gatherings in order to refute any false teaching he might hear. But it was not long before the large-hearted curate realized his mistake. Nervously at first, Grimshaw began to seek out the pedlar and many were the issues the two men discussed, often in some secret rendezvous on the moors above Haworth.

An uncommon friendship soon sprang up between the two. A rugged and unconventional person himself, Grimshaw was able to appreciate the fearless Scotsman. But more than this, Grimshaw's own spiritual experience was often clouded through lack of a strong assurance of faith, and Darney, well-taught in the Scriptures and a convinced Calvinist, proved an invaluable help to him. It was a debt Grimshaw never forgot. At last he began to support Darney publicly, even giving out the hymns and praying at his services. 'Mad Grimshaw is turned Scotch Will's clerk,' the people began to say, as the spiritual benefits of his new-found assurance added a fresh dimension of power to Grimshaw's preaching.

In a letter written to Dr John Gillies in 1754, Grimshaw catalogues the progress of the revival in the north of England and readily ascribes the rapid expansion of the gospel throughout the area to the endeavours of his friend William Darney: 'In the year 1746, by this man [Darney] the Lord pushed the work westwards. Great numbers in the next parish {Heptonstall]were awakened and brought to the knowledge of Jesus. Lancashire now received the first revival. Pendle Forest, Colne parish, Todmorden, Rossendale... were visited by the Lord and many brought to acknowledge his free redeeming and saving power.'

The Heptonstall Octagon, the oldest Methodist chapel still in use today, bears on its foundation-stone a silent tribute to the effective witness of this zealous preacher.

By 1747 Darney felt the need for an improved spiritual oversight for the little groups of converts from his ministry. After some hesitation he approached John Wesley, asking him to accept responsibility for them. Reluctantly at first, Wesley agreed and added Darney's name to his list of accredited preachers. But it was an uneasy alliance, and Darney was constantly incurring the disfavour of the Wesley brothers. His vibrant Calvinism troubled John Wesley, the more so when he insisted on raising controversial issues among Wesley's converts; while his doggerel hymns, which he continued to compose and teach to the people, offended Charles Wesley's poetic ear. But Darney had a friend whom he knew would stand by him. Whenever he was in trouble with the Wesley brothers and was consequently struck off their list of preachers—as happened on a number of occasions—he would then resort to Grimshaw for help. Grimshaw, in whom both the Wesleys placed much confidence, would plead his cause until John Wesley had reinstated Scotch Will.

During this period Darney gave himself entirely to his preaching, having no source of income apart from the contributions made by the societies to whom he preached. Poor indeed he was, especially as he had a wife and family to support, and throughout these years we read in the Methodist circuit books such entries as: 'Jan. 10 1749—A pair of boots for W.D.— £0 14s 0d.'

But Darney was a stalwart trail-blazer and readily travelled to areas where no messenger of the gospel had yet ventured. Not only did he open up Lancashire to the gospel, but he was also responsible for pioneering vast tracts of north Yorkshire and Cumbria. Wherever he went, he aroused strong emotions: he was loved by those who gladly received the transforming truth, but hated by representatives of established religion into whose territory he penetrated. Repeatedly these ungodly clerics would inflame a turbulent mob both to mock and injure the bold preacher. At Osmotherley, in north Yorkshire, Scotch Will was daubed with tar and then ridiculed still more by being decorated with feathers. Far from allowing such treatment to prevent his return, there are records of his further preaching there, accompanied by his equally courageous friend William Grimshaw in 1752.

In Alnwick, near the Scottish border, the work of God prospered, but as ever, this aroused both hostility and insult. A local troupe of actors decided to put on a skit caricaturing Darney. Bills were distributed for the show, but before the play was performed, Darney rode past the actors as they relaxed near their theatre. 'Here is Scotch Will!' they cried merrily. 'Let's mob him!''But Darney, a man of impressive size, was also riding a highly-spirited horse, and on hearing the threat, he cantered up to them. Rearing his animal up on its hind legs, he roared with a crack of his whip, 'Come on, ye sons of Belial!' Terrified, the actors promised to cancel the show.

However, Darney frequently tasted the full frenzy of mob violence. Once he was thrust into the local jail. On another occasion his coat, a garment he could ill afford to replace, was ruined by being dipped in a vat of dye. Barrowford, a village near Colne in Lancashire, was the scene of repeated persecution of the Methodist preachers. Here too William Darney was ill-treated when the drunken mob threw him into the river, which flowed through the village in a deep gully ten feet below the road level. Not satisfied with this cruelty, one of their number scrambled in after him, mounted his back, cast a bridle around his head and rode him like a horse. Cheered on by spectators, he was forced to swim into the deepest part of the river. Finally they tied a rope round his waist and fastened the ends to opposite banks, making it impossible for him to wade out until one of his friends rescued him. In Colne itself he was further degraded by being stripped of his clothing, rolled in mud and driven through the main street.

But, as we have seen, it was not always the enemies of truth that prevailed. Once the ringleader of an angry crowd lunged forward to drag Darney from his makeshift pulpit. Grabbing him by his cravat, the man was astonished when the material tore easily in his hand, leaving the preacher unscathed. Nervously he assumed that this was a divine intervention to save Darney from his hands, and the incident led to his conversion from a persecutor to a penitent sinner.

Nor were Darney's antagonists his only source of trouble. Road conditions could become treacherous after heavy rain, and sometimes his horse would stumble and throw him off into marshy ground, causing him injury, or, at the least, discomfort. Once when he was drenched to the skin after such an accident, his friends took him to a nearby farmhouse where they asked if the preacher might dry his clothes by the fire. Much to the farmer's surprise, his bedraggled visitor did not immediately avail himself of his kindness. Instead he said simply, 'Let us pray.' Kneeling down in the farmer's kitchen, Darney poured out his heart in prayer to God. Then he rose from his knees, strode restlessly to and fro, and said once more, 'Let us pray.'

Amazed and deeply affected by this unexpected behaviour, the farmer said, 'You shall not leave my house this night, for there is something in you which I never saw in any man before.'

'Say you so?' responded the preacher, 'then go and invite all your neighbours and I will preach to them.'

Whether Darney dried his clothes before his congregation arrived we are not told. Suffice it to say that the power of God so accompanied his words that the farmer and many who heard him were awakened to their spiritual condition.

In the years that followed we catch glimpses of William Darney as he laboured in different parts of the country at John Wesley's direction. In 1762 he must have rejoiced at being sent to Haworth to work with his friend William Grimshaw.

Financially, too, his position was improving to some degree as the itinerant preachers were then being given a modest amount of support. So the records for January 1763 reveal that Darney himself received £3. 5s. for the first quarter of the year, while for the upkeep of his horse he was granted £3. 1s. 7d.

After Grimshaw's death in 1763, Scotch Will had no one to take his part with the Wesley brothers when he offended against their protocol. Controversial and outspoken though he was, the abundant blessing of God rested on him, and when he was sent far off from the scenes of his life's labours to preach in Cornwall a first-hand report describes the results; 'The work of God more or less prospered in every society in the county. In two or three months hundreds were added to the societies in the west, and many savingly brought to the knowledge of the Lord Jesus Christ. Many backsliders were restored, and a most wonderful change took place in every parish where the gospel was preached. Most of the country villages were like Eden, and as the garden of the Lord! It was not uncommon for ten or twenty to find peace with God in one day, or at one sermon or love feast.'

Not surprisingly, such demonstrations of God's power soon attracted the assaults of Satan, who sowed dissension among the men whom God was using. Darney's strength of conviction, accompanied by his frequent lack of wisdom, provided the occasion for disaffection. 'For a season he behaved pretty well,' wrote a fellow preacher, 'and was ready to be advised; but he relapsed into his former conduct, and advanced opinions in public contrary to Methodist doctrine and discipline, so we were obliged to call in a young man to labour in his place and dismiss him from the circuit, and that by Mr Wesley's express approbation.'

Apart from Darney's staunch Calvinism, which constantly worried Wesley, the issues which most commonly caused a breach between Darney and his fellow workers were twofold. Wesley's emphasis on Christian perfection, which taught that a believer might be sanctified by an act of appropriating faith and be wholly delivered from known sin in this life, did not ring true to Darney's understanding of the Scriptures. On the other hand, Darney's own confident assurance that all true believers would persevere to the last added a further source of contention between the two men. 'I shall either mend William Darney, or end him. He must not go on in this manner,' was Wesley's own cryptic comment on Darney's outbursts from time to time. And end him he did.

With none to plead his cause, and cut off from Wesley's list of preachers, Darney returned to the north of England. Occasional references to him in the chronicles of the times indicate that he continued preaching. In 1766 he was in Yarn, near Stockton; the following year he had moved further north to Newcastle, and in

1768 he had once more travelled as far south as Derbyshire. With no other means of support, we may suppose that he now resumed his rounds as a pedlar.

Frail and elderly, William Darney visited Almondbury, near Huddersfield, in 1770, where, as we have seen, he once again experienced the mad fury of a mob incited to violence by a local cleric. At his first meeting with the society in that place he discovered only seven believers gathering for fellowship. Within a month that number had grown to thirty-two, which excited the anger of the vicar, who regarded the itinerant preacher as an intruder into his territory. Trouble began when the parish clerk arrived on the scene after Darney had finished preaching and requested a word with him. Innocently the Scotsman was about to comply, when his friends, surmising that trouble lay in store, grabbed his coat to prevent him from proceeding. A furious tussle ensued in which Darney's coat was ripped to pieces, for what Darney did not realize, but his friends had guessed, was that waiting outside was an enraged mob of locals ready to lynch him.

The following week, when the intrepid preacher returned to Almondbury, he did not escape the full force of the brutality of the crowd, which as recounted earlier, nearly cost him his life.

To avoid the repetition of such scenes, the society began to meet at five o'clock in the morning each Sunday, and one who recalled those days in old age wrote, 'How did we then love each other! How glad we were to see each other! And how happy we were when we met together!'

After a life full of sufferings, Darney, weakened by all the physical ill-treatment he had endured, moved to the Pendle Forest area of Lancashire, which resembled the beauties of his own homeland. Long after his death in 1779 locals could recall this Boanerges of the revival as a feeble, white-haired old man who walked each week to a nearby farm to buy threepence worth of butter.

But William Darney's best obituary is found in his own words: 'I have known by happy experience, that when I have been in the greatest extremity of sufferings for my dear Lord and Master's sake, when I have been preaching in several places... when I did not expect to escape with my life, God in rich mercy, and in his great wisdom, and mighty power, made always a way for my escape. I say, I have found in the greatest extremity of suffering, always most of God's presence, when the sons of wickedness have been permitted to abuse my body, and tear my clothes in pieces. Yet my soul at the same time was like a watered garden... I have at times tasted of the martyrs' cup, praised be my God who counted unworthy me worthy of this honour, for his name and gospel's sake. There was one time in particular, when the persecutors had taken me and tumbled me head over ears in a nasty hole full of mire, with my enemies dancing and pushing one another on top of me. Indeed, I was infinitely more happy in that hole than all my enemies could have been if they had been lying on beds of down, for there my soul did lean upon my Beloved's breast. I found such a manifestation of God's love ... [that I] felt something of the heaven of heavens in my soul.'

Harriet Newell: Where stormy seas cannot divide

Harriet, wife of Samuel Newell, was only eighteen when she and her husband sailed to India with Adoniram and Nancy Judson in 1812. These two couples were the first American missionaries to serve under the auspices of the American Board of Foreign Missions, formed in 1810 to meet the growing awareness among American Christians of the need for missionary endeavour.

It came as a shock to seventeen-year-old Harriet Atwood when she learnt that her friend Nancy Hasseltine had agreed to marry Adoniram Judson. She and Nancy had been friends since their days together at Bradford Academy in Massachusetts, where both girls had been deeply influenced by a work of the Spirit of God that had swept through the academy in 1806. Harriet was thirteen at the time and had held Nancy, three years her senior, in high regard.

Nancy's engagement to Judson held far-reaching consequences, for he was one of a group of five young men who had dedicated their lives to the cause of reaching the unevangelized multitudes in India and the East with the gospel of Christ. These were to be the first American missionaries; their ardour and vision had profoundly stirred the hearts and consciences of American Christians. And now Nancy Hasseltine was to marry one of them, exchanging home and friends for a life of hardship and sufferings. Harriet recorded in her secret diary: 'How did this news affect my heart! Is she willing to do all this for God and shall I refuse to lend my little aid?'

Born in Haverhill, Massachusetts, in 1793, Harriet was a lively, outgoing girl, with a cheerful disposition. One of a family of nine, her love for reading and a retentive memory marked her out as a child of some natural ability. This encouraged her parents to send Harriet to the Academy of Bradford to continue her education when she was thirteen. Light-hearted by nature, Harriet had given little time or thought to eternal issues before attending the academy, though her early training gave her a twinge of conscience from time to time. Then the girl would try to be more dutiful in repeating her prayers and reading the Scriptures.

But all this was to change in 1806. An unusual work of God in the town of Bradford soon began to affect the girls at the academy. Yet while others were beginning to show deep concern for their souls, Harriet remained outwardly heedless, fearing to incur the ridicule of her companions. For three months she struggled against God's Spirit, refusing to consider the implications of her careless way of life. But at last she was drawn to seek forgiveness with a twofold cord: the infinite attractiveness of the character and person of Christ, and a fear of the awesome consequences of unbelief.

Not for another three years, however, did Harriet begin to show any marked growth in grace. Looking back, she was to confess that soon after the immediate impact of the revival had passed, her zeal and concern abated. The Bible, once so precious, was scarcely opened, while romances and novels held her spellbound. But she was not happy: a day of spiritual neglect would lead to the accusations of a burdened conscience, followed in turn by many a troubled night. Not even the death of her father from tuberculosis when Harriet was only fifteen, though it distressed the girl, awakened her again, either to seek God's consolations, or to fulfil his righteous demands. But God's moment was soon to come, and a sermon which Harriet heard in June 1809 melted her heart in penitence and love for the Saviour. Now she could write, 'I then made the solemn resolution in the strength of Jesus that I would make a sincere dedication of my all to my Creator for time and eternity.'

Scarcely was the ink dry on Harriet's paper before the sincerity of her resolve was tested by one of her closest friends who wished to draw Harriet back again to her former course of life. This time she overcame her fear of the opinions of others and challenged the friend over her neglect of God.

Applying to become a communicant member of her church at Haverhill, Harriet marked her new determination by entering into the required public covenant with God and with the church, undertaking to endeavour to turn from a life of worldliness and live in devotion to Christ.

But these things were to be put to a far more searching test the following year when Harriet first heard of her friend Nancy's decision to marry Adoniram Judson. Judson's eager willingness for missionary service, together with that of three other students from Andover Theological Seminary, all by the name of Samuel— Samuel Newell, Samuel Nott and Samuel Mills (later joined by a fifth student) had stunned American Christians. It had brought a new awareness in the churches of the plight of the vast bulk of the earth's population, living and dying in a state of spiritual darkness and destitution. Harriet expressed the feelings of many when she recorded in her journal for 20 October 1810: 'I have felt more for the salvation of the heathen this day than I can recollect to have felt through my whole past life... They are perishing for lack of knowledge, while I enjoy the glorious privileges of a Christian land. Great God, direct me! Oh make me in some way beneficial to their immortal souls!'

Little did Harriet know as she penned those words that within three days this challenge would become yet more pressing and personal. On 23 October she was introduced to Samuel Newell, another of the missionary volunteers. An immediate bond sprang up between them, and within a week Newell was back in the Atwood home. He and Harriet spoke together at length. 'He gave me some account of the dealings of God with his soul,' wrote Harriet, adding, 'He is willing to renounce his earthly happiness for the interest of religion.'

But Harriet fought against the implications of the young missionary candidate's interest in her. Since the death of her father two years earlier, her mother had become increasingly dependent on her eldest daughter's support. In addition, Harriet was far from strong herself, suffering from frequent migraine headaches and also a tendency to bronchitis. So Samuel's repeated visits to Haverhill both thrilled and alarmed Harriet. And then, six months later, in April 1811, a friend handed her a sealed envelope. Recognizing the handwriting, she scarcely dared open it. Its contents threw the girl into immediate turmoil. 'This was not a long-wished-for letter,' she wrote in her journal. 'No, it was a long-dreaded one.' Should she marry Newell and 'consent to leave for ever the friends of my life, the dear scenes of my childhood and go to a land of strangers?' she pondered anxiously. Nor was he allowing her a long period of reflection on his offer of marriage. Funds were coming in for the proposed mission and a suitable ship travelling to India, providing adequate accommodation for the missionary recruits, might become available at short notice. 'Oh for direction from heaven!' Harriet cried.

Two days passed and still the girl was in an emotional and spiritual turmoil. 'What shall I do?' she asked rhetorically in the pages of her journal. 'If tears could direct me in the path of duty, surely I should be directed. My heart aches. I know not what to do! Guide me, O thou great Jehovah.'

Perhaps her mother would resolve the crisis, Harriet thought, by refusing to allow her to go on the grounds of her age—for she was still only seventeen—her health and her own need of her child. 'If this should be the case,' wrote Harriet piously, 'my duty would be plain.' But Harriet's mother was prepared to sacrifice her child. 'If a conviction of duty and love to the souls of the perishing heathen lead you to India, as much as I love you, Harriet, I can only say, "Go,"' she had replied.

With her last excuse stripped away, and her increasing love for the zealous missionary candidate, Harriet married Samuel Newell towards the end of 1811, not long after she had turned eighteen. Weeks of preparation followed as they made final arrangements for a journey which would take them far from home and friends for ever. Although they knew they must be ready to travel at any time, it still came as a shock when news broke that the brig *Caravan* was sailing in February and would take the two married missionaries with their wives to India.

Emotional farewell scenes followed for Adoniram and Nancy Judson, and Harriet and Samuel Newell as the small trading ship finally set sail from Salem on 19 February 1812. Heavily laden with merchandise, because impending war with England could prohibit further voyages, the ship also carried a large supply of provisions for the voyage, including live pigs and chickens to supply the crew and the four passengers with fresh meat.

Harriet felt the separation keenly. Embracing a life of unknown dangers, she knew she had no realistic hope of ever seeing her family again. Within a week their lives were thrown into danger when the vessel sprang a leak that was only repaired with difficulty. In addition seasickness, cramped conditions and a limited diet increased their discomfort; but for Harriet there were also the problems of early pregnancy, for she was now expecting her first child. As longings for the comforts of home swept over the young woman, her thoughts turned to the heavenly city when partings would end for ever. 'There is a land, my dear mother,' she wrote, 'where stormy seas cannot divide the friends of Jesus. There I hope to meet you and all my beloved friends to whom on earth I have bid adieu. Oh that Harriet, an exile in a distant land, with her mother, brothers and sisters, may be united in the family of the Most High in heaven!'

Week after week passed by as the small vessel steered its course around the Cape of Good Hope. On into the Indian Ocean they sailed, with only the infinity of sea and sky to greet their eyes. 'I care not how soon we reach Calcutta,' wrote Harriet one day. 'I have been so weary of the excessive rocking of the vessel, and the almost intolerable smell after the rain that I have done little more than lounge on the bed for several days. But I have been blest with excellent spirits.'

By early June the *Caravan* was at last approaching India after four months at sea. A pilot came on board to guide the brig safely through the Ganges delta into Calcutta harbour, but before reaching their destination there were still perils to encounter. When darkness fell they had cast anchor, but heavy seas rolled the vessel from side to side, driving them back to the open sea, while the waves flooded their tiny cabins. Harriet described the conditions in her journal: 'The vessel rocked violently all the evening... About eleven o'clock the cable broke and we were dashed about all night... The anchor was lost yet we were preserved from a sudden and awful death by the God who rules the seas.'

Eventually on 17 June the sea-weary party disembarked safely and were delighted to find William Carey himself in Calcutta. Carried aloft in palanquins, the American missionaries were taken to Carey's cool, second-floor office, where they met the bronzed, unpretentious missionary who welcomed them cordially and invited them to stay in Serampore until their future was decided. Harriet described the occasion: 'We were affectionately received by the good Dr Carey at his mansion in Calcutta and treated with the greatest hospitality... Imagine a small bald-headed man of sixty: such is the one whose name will be remembered to the latest generation. He is now advanced to a state of honour... We accepted his invitation to visit the missionary family at Serampore.'

Travelling by boat to Serampore the following day, the new missionaries were greeted by Joshua Marshman, William Ward and their wives, and were astonished as they were shown round the extensive mission complex. Harriet was relieved and delighted by the spacious accommodation where they were to live. She felt an immediate affection for Mrs Ward, whose motherly heart had gone out to the pregnant eighteen-year-old. 'I love dear Mrs Ward more and more every day,' she recorded. 'She is remarkably kind to us. I go to her constantly for advice.'

But their stay in India was short-lived. Never a friend of missions, the British East India Company was particularly antagonistic towards American missionaries. Renewed hostilities had just broken out between America and England and the four fresh arrivals were peremptorily ordered to return to America on the very ship which had brought them to India. The captain would not be granted clearance for his vessel to sail until all four were back on board. Frantic negotiations followed. Marshman and Carey did all in their power to have the mandate reversed. Harriet was deeply depressed at the situation: 'How dark and intricate are the ways of Providence!' she wrote. 'We are ordered by government to leave the British territories and return to America immediately... thus are all our prospects blasted... Must we be the instruments of discouraging all American Christians to give these nations the Word of Life? My spirit faints within me. These are trials great and unexpected.'

At last a compromise was reached: the Americans were to be allowed to sail to Mauritius on a goods vessel, the *Gillespie*, instead of home on the *Caravan*. But further complications arose when the captain of the *Gillespie* would only agree to take one of the couples. With Harriet's baby due within three months, the choice was clear and by the end of July, only five weeks after their arrival, she and Samuel had boarded the ship carrying them far from the land where they had hoped to serve their God. Harriet felt the disappointment acutely. The prospect of another long voyage back across the Indian Ocean was daunting, particularly as she would be the only woman on board. But she still managed to write cheerfully to her mother, 'I go without one female companion; but I go with renewed courage, rejoicing that the Lord has opened us a way to work for him.'

Exhausted by hasty preparations for their departure, and an enervating round of farewells, Harriet was ill for the first week of the voyage. For three further weeks the vessel was tossed to and fro in the Bay of Bengal, making little progress towards its destination. Eventually, like the *Caravan*, it sprang a leak, throwing the whole ship's company into imminent danger. Not before 19 September was it once more ready to sail for Mauritius. Harriet's confinement was now imminent and it was becoming increasingly doubtful whether she would reach Mauritius and medical help in time.

We may only guess at the young woman's anxieties as it became evident that her little one would be born at sea. But her trust in God remained steadfast: 'I know that God orders everything in the best possible manner. If he so orders events that I suffer pain and sickness on the stormy ocean without a female friend, shall I repine and think he deals hardly with me?' And on 9 October, a day before her nineteenth birthday, with no one but her husband present to help, Harriet gave birth to a baby daughter whom they also called Harriet.

But four days later the ship ran into a fierce storm. Powerful winds tossed the vessel about, while mountainous waves crashed over it, drenching all on board. Baby Harriet caught a severe chill which quickly turned to pneumonia. 'About 8 o'clock last evening our dear little Harriet died in her mother's arms,' wrote Samuel sorrowfully. 'A sweet child. Though she had been but five days with us it was painful, inexpressibly painful, especially to the mother, to part with her. Today with many tears we committed her to a watery grave. So fades the lovely blooming flower.' Then with both faith and foreboding, Samuel added, 'May God sanctify this bereavement to us, and, oh! may he spare my dear wife!'

But it was not to be. Weak from her confinement, worn with grief at her loss, Harriet too had caught a chill and soon began to show symptoms of tuberculosis. With a predisposition to chest infections and having watched her father die of this condition, she entertained little hope of recovery. Heaven became a bright reality, where she would be freed from the bonds of sin and sorrow. As the *Gillespie* docked at last, Samuel hoped that medical attention would yet save his Harriet. But her illness was far advanced. 'Tell my dear mother how much Harriet loved her. Tell her to look to God and keep near to him. I shall meet her in heaven,' she whispered when her strength seemed almost gone. For her brothers and sisters she also had a message. 'Let my dear brothers and sisters know that I loved them to the last,' she said with tears streaming down her cheeks. 'Tell them from the lips of their dying sister that there is nothing but religion worth living for.' And to Samuel she said, 'Jesus will be your best friend and our separation will be short.' Asked how her past life appeared to her, she replied, 'Bad enough; but that only makes the grace of Christ appear more glorious.'

On 30 November, six weeks after her baby's death, this brave young missionary was called to serve her God in a better land. A broken-hearted letter from Samuel to Harriet's mother describes his loss: 'Have courage, my mother. God will support you under this trial, though it may for a time cause your very heart to bleed. Come then, let us mingle our griefs and weep together; for she was dear to us both, and she is gone. Yes, Harriet, your lovely daughter is gone, and you will see her face no more. Harriet, my own dear Harriet, the wife of my youth and the desire of my eyes, has bid me a last farewell, and left me to mourn and weep. Yes, she is gone. I saw her ascend to the mansions of the blessed! Oh Harriet, Harriet, for thou wast very dear to me. Thy last sigh tore my heart in sunder, and dissolved the chain which tied me to earth.'

Samuel himself only lived another six years, serving as a missionary in Bombay, before he once more joined his Harriet in the heavenly country—that land where stormy seas could no more divide. Such was the heroism and sacrifice of these first missionaries.

Ezekiel Rogers:
God's poor exile

During the reigns of James I and Charles I, in the period prior to the English Civil War which broke out in 1642, Christians who felt unable to comply with the restrictions placed on their consciences by the prelates of the day faced an agonizing choice. Either they must conform, or endure heavy penalties for their nonconformity. Many, however, chose a third option and decided to emigrate to the New World. This was the course chosen by Ezekiel Rogers.

Rowley Manor in Yorkshire is an idyllic venue for a wedding reception. Approached along a tree-lined glade, its spacious rooms and sweeping lawns surrounded by peaceful pastureland convey an air of tranquillity. But it was not always so. If we were to travel back in time some three hundred and sixty years, a far different picture would greet us. The vicarage, built where Rowley Manor now stands, was astir with activity. And not only there, but throughout the village of Rowley, we would discover scenes of frantic bustle as family after family gathered together all the possessions they could carry in preparation for a journey — a journey fraught with dangers and uncertainties that would take them far from their familiar Yorkshire countryside to distant New England.

When Ezekiel Rogers first began his ministry at the Rowley parish church of St Peter in 1616, he discovered a people living out their days in ignorance of the God who made them. Governed by superstitions and the fear of death, they listened with astonishment to the message proclaimed to them by their young parson, a man only twenty-six years of age. But in the years that followed a change so profound was to take place in Rowley and the surrounding area that when persecution silenced their preacher twenty years later the whole village was prepared to emigrate rather than lose the blessings of the Word of Life.

Ezekiel Rogers, son of Richard Rogers of Wethersfield and cousin of the better-known John Rogers of Dedham in Essex, was born in 1590. From an early age he had shown a degree of ability which encouraged his father to secure him a place at Cambridge at the age of thirteen. Graduating with his MA degree at the age of twenty, Ezekiel gained maturity as he spent some years as chaplain and tutor in the family of Sir Francis Barrington of Hatfield in Essex. Here he cultivated his social skills as he had regular opportunity to mix with the nobility of the day. And here also the young man began to develop his own considerable talent as a preacher.

Throughout his formative years Ezekiel had listened to the preaching of his eminently gifted and godly father, who was known as the 'Enoch' of his day, both for his walk with God and for the spiritual effectiveness of his preaching. Coming from such a background, Ezekiel had both a natural and an acquired facility with words and soon expressed a wish to enter the ministry himself. His eloquence in public prayer and his persuasiveness in the pulpit proved more than sufficient recommendation and, after six years in Hatfield, Sir Francis presented his young chaplain with the living of St Peter in the village of Rowley, in rural Yorkshire.

The parish church, lying ten miles west of Hull, served not only the local community, but was a focal point for many of the nearby Yorkshire hamlets and farmsteads. Rogers' congregation would arrive on horseback from Little Weighton, Hunsley, Bentley, Wallington and even Cottingham. As news of the preaching of the new vicar spread throughout the community, the numbers attending began to climb. Soon the initial astonishment among his hearers gave place to concern. The people were profoundly affected by the passionate appeals of this preacher who urged on them the necessity of contrition of heart for sin and conversion to God.

But Ezekiel Rogers had not been long at Rowley before the realization began to grow upon him that he himself was still a stranger to those very experiences which he so eloquently pressed upon his parishioners. Had he ever known that personal repentance for his sins, or that inward joy springing from an assurance of the forgiveness of God of which he preached? What should he do? To whom could he go? He knew of no one locally who would be able to help him. His anxiety deepened and he trembled as he thought of the final end of the hypocrite.

At last his distress became so acute that he knew it was imperative that he seek out someone with whom he could speak. His father had recently died, and so Ezekiel's mind turned to his cousin John Rogers in Essex. Described as 'one of the most awakening preachers of the age,' John Rogers was exercising a ministry that was attracting hearers from a wide area around Dedham.

Gladly Ezekiel saddled his horse and rode the two hundred or more miles along ill-made and dangerous roads in order to resolve his spiritual crisis. He had hoped to see his cousin in private, but on arriving in Dedham, he discovered a service in progress and decided he must join the congregation. John Rogers, sometimes known as 'Roaring Rogers' because of the power with which he preached, did not notice his cousin slip into the church. As Ezekiel listened earnestly to the sermon, the Spirit of God applied the words to his troubled conscience. Light and peace flooded his mind. Although he no doubt spent some time with his cousin, he no longer needed to seek out his help. All Ezekiel's perplexities were resolved, for at last he knew of a certainty that he too had entered the kingdom of heaven through repentance and faith.

Returning to Rowley with a glad heart, Rogers began his ministry at St Peter's once more. But though the words might have been the same, now they were accompanied by a power and effectiveness he had never known before. Men and women were moved and converted through his ministry. News of the remarkable events in Rowley spread throughout the community, and the people began to stream into the village to hear the message preached in the parish church.

For many years Ezekiel Rogers conducted an effective ministry in the village and far beyond. Yorkshire had been one of the least favoured parts of England for a testimony to the truth among the people. Now men and women would travel from other parts of the county to hear Rogers preach—some from as far away as York, or even occasionally from Leeds or Bradford. For seventeen years, spanning the troubled period prior to the Civil War, he conducted his ministry unmolested, even while Archbishop Laud's regime was silencing many other good men who refused to compromise their evangelical principles.

This was due largely to the encouragement and support Rogers received from Dr Tobias Matthews, Archbishop of York, who was sympathetic to the message he preached. More than this, the kindly archbishop allowed him to conduct monthly 'lectures' in different parts of the county. These lectures, inaugurated by Archbishop Edmund Grindal in the previous century, were in reality preaching meetings and were an indirect means of increasing the occasions for gospel ministry, so bringing the light of the Word of God to many country areas.

But such gatherings also stirred up opposition. A fellow clergyman, jealous of the favour Rogers enjoyed with the archbishop, once approached the prelate privately and complained that during the course of one of Rogers' lectures someone had prayed, 'May the Almighty shut heaven against the archbishop's grace.' Expecting that such an apparently imprecatory prayer would bring about Rogers' downfall, the talebearer was not a little disconcerted when Matthews broke into hearty laughter, and exclaimed, 'Those good men know well enough that if I were gone to heaven, their exercises would soon be put down.'

And so it proved. For after Matthews' death in 1628 a new Archbishop of York was appointed who was hostile to Puritan principles and determined to make the errant vicar of St Peter's conform or resign. Slowly and subtly, Rogers' freedom was restricted. First the monthly lectures were closed down. Then after 1633 the restrictions placed on him grew more pronounced until a crisis came in 1636 when all incumbents were required to read to their congregations from the 'Book of Sports'—a treatise legalizing the practice of using Sunday for many types of sport and recreation. This Ezekiel Rogers was unwilling to do. For him the issues were clear—either he must conform or relinquish his living. He chose the latter.

Deprived of their preacher, the people of Rowley were bewildered and distressed. Rogers himself was permitted to appoint his successor, but this man too was quickly suspended for his refusal to read a public censure of his predecessor. For two years Rogers remained in Rowley but was prohibited from conducting any ministry. At last he saw no alternative but to leave his homeland and emigrate to New England in search of liberty to worship and preach in accordance with his understanding of God's Word. When his people heard that their pastor, his wife Joan and their family were packing all their possessions in order to emigrate, the entire village decided that, rather than lose the messenger whose preaching had meant more than life to them, they would accompany him.

So it was that one morning in 1638 all the people of Rowley were to be seen stacking their belongings into wagons—farming implements, kitchen utensils, furniture, clothing, as much as the restricted conditions on the ship would permit them to carry. Included in Ezekiel Rogers' own luggage was his highly-valued library and a printing-press—said to have been the first press taken to New England.

Whips cracked and the wagons trundled off on their ten-mile trek into Hull, leaving behind a ghost village—the quiet homes of Rowley never to be occupied again. Passing into the old city of Hull through the Beverley Gate and down Whitefriargate—now a pedestrianized thoroughfare—they rattled on down the busy, cobbled High Street until they reached the River Hull. Among the congested vessels moored along the banks of this narrow waterway lay a small merchant ship named *The John*, which the villagers of Rowley had chartered. Unloading their possessions, these exiles for conscience' sake boarded *The John* and set sail for the New World.

A hazardous voyage under cramped conditions followed for the Yorkshire congregation. Families with lively children, and even newborn babies, endured the privations of the voyage for more than three months until at last the ship cast anchor in Massachusetts Bay.

Travelling north with all their possessions, the Rowley villagers were allocated land which they could cultivate and form into a settlement. And what better name could they give to their new home than Rowley? Here, amid all the hardships and dangers from disease, failed crops and marauding Indians, Ezekiel Rogers ministered to his people once more with all his customary encouragement and spiritual challenge. As in Rowley, Yorkshire, so in Rowley, New England, his ministry was owned by God and soon many were clamouring to hear him preach. So perceptive was he of the needs and condition of his ever-increasing congregation that his hearers would suspect that someone had been informing their pastor of their inmost thoughts and secret sins.

Never a strong man, Rogers suffered frequent ill-health throughout his life. The nervous energy expended in preaching would often exhaust him; sometimes it seemed the sword was too sharp for its scabbard and Rogers would experience periods of debility which kept him from his pulpit. Distrustful of the medics of his day, he took up the study of medicine himself and often advised his people, not only on the concerns of their souls, but also on coping with their common ailments. Known as a peacemaker, Rogers would find himself sought out by the settlers of New England, with their seemingly irreconcilable differences, and frequently he would resolve the problems.

For a further twenty-two years Ezekiel Rogers ministered in the second Rowley. He was a favourite with the children of his parish and his home was always open to them. Sometimes a dozen or more would crowd into his large kitchen in the evening and listen, fascinated, to the anecdotes he would tell. But always he mingled his stories with serious exhortations, urging them to read good books, give time to prayer and be watchful against temptation.

That such admonitions were timely is apparent from a letter, preserved from Rogers' correspondence to a fellow minister, in which he laments the manifest lack of godliness among the young people of New England: 'I find greatest grief and trouble about the rising generation. Young people are little stirred here, but they strengthen one another in evil... Even the children of the godly make woeful proof. So that I tremble to think what will become of this glorious work we have begun when the ancient shall be gathered unto their fathers. I fear grace and blessing will die with them.'

The last years of Ezekiel Rogers' life were hard indeed. First came discord within his own congregation. Because his ministry was becoming increasingly acknowledged and blessed, he was persuaded to set up 'lectures,' similar in style to those he had conducted in Yorkshire. This in turn led to the necessity for an assistant pastor to ease the burden on Rogers, who was now approaching sixty years of age. A gifted young preacher was appointed to the position, but the people became divided in their loyalties, and the peace of the church was broken by jealousy and suspicions.

Divisions were healed and misunderstandings smoothed over, but damage had been done, and the death of his faithful wife Joan in 1649 left Rogers bereft indeed. Like him, she had been a voluntary exile from her homeland for the gospel's sake, and had shared with him all the hazards of his chosen course. Shortly after their mother's death each of his children died one by one until he alone was left, bereaved of all domestic comfort. Feeling the need of love and companionship, Rogers remarried. But his new bride, a young woman, died shortly afterwards together with the infant she had lately borne him.

A third marriage, contracted with a Mary Barker, widow of one of his Yorkshire parishioners who had sailed with him in 1638, also began in adversity. The very night after the wedding had been celebrated his home, built largely of wood, caught fire and was totally destroyed, together with all his furniture, clothes and, most grievously of all, the valuable library which he had brought with him from Rowley in Yorkshire. And as if these afflictions were not enough, a fall from his horse so dislocated his right arm that it became paralysed, forcing Rogers to learn to write with his left hand.

But in all his distresses Ezekiel Rogers experienced inner consolations from God and was marked by a cheerful spirit. Approaching his seventieth year, asthmatic and far from well, he looked with anticipation to the joys of heaven. Writing to a friend with his left hand, he expressed his hopes in these words: 'I am hastening home, and grow very asthmatical and short-breathed. Oh, that I might see some signs of good to the generations following to send me away rejoicing! ... Oh, good brother, I thank God I am near home, and you too are not far. Oh, the weight of glory that is ready waiting for us, God's poor exiles! We shall sit next to the martyrs and confessors. Oh, the embraces wherewith Christ will embrace us! Cheer up your spirits in the thoughts thereof, and let us be zealous for our God and Christ and make a conclusion. Now the Lord bring us well through our poor pilgrimage.'

And so in 1660, at the age of seventy, 'God's poor exile' finished his pilgrimage and joined those noble men and women of faith who had gone before. Words on his gravestone read:

A resurrection to Immortality is here expected for what was mortal of the Reverend EZEKIEL ROGERS. Put off, January 23 1660.

Jane: A child who believed

Known only as 'Jane,' this twelve-year-old girl was an early convert of Rev. Legh Richmond's ministry on the Isle of Wight which began in 1797. Her story is more fully told in The Dairyman's Daughter, *a book which became popular reading during the nineteenth century.*

Twelve-year-old Jane was one of a group of young people who came each Saturday afternoon to Legh Richmond's home shortly after he began his ministry in Brading on the Isle of Wight in 1797.

Some of the children seemed bright and responsive as he taught them from the Scriptures and by means of questions and answers from the catechism. Jane, on the other hand, who was a quiet, plain-looking child, seemed notable for little more than her regular attendance and scarcely attracted the minister's attention. Struggling at first with her reading, she slowly gained confidence and as the months passed began to answer the questions he posed with tolerable accuracy. But had Richmond been asked which of the children showed the most promise, Jane's name would have been at the bottom of the list, or not even mentioned at all.

On some sunny afternoons Richmond would take the class into his garden and teach them under the shade of a tree. Just beyond the garden fence lay the churchyard. Here villagers had been buried for many generations. Some graves were marked only by a simple inscription; others bore a more elaborate epitaph, often in verse. Sometimes he would send his class into the graveyard to study the words engraved on the headstones, pointing out that many of the graves belonged to children and that, therefore, they too must be prepared for death. 'Where do you expect your soul will go after you die?' he would enquire as the children gathered around some small grave.

One day he asked his class to memorize the verses of an epitaph which he thought remarkable. Each child returned and repeated the words to him, but when Jane came back he was amazed to hear her say that she had also memorized the words of another inscription which she had discovered on the next stone. Four of its eight lines read:

> Hail! glorious gospel, heavenly light, whereby
> We live with comfort and with comfort die;
> And view beyond this gloomy scene and tomb,
> A life of endless happiness to come.

But the incident soon passed from Richmond's mind. Neither did he notice Jane's absence from the group during the following weeks, or even from the Sunday services at Brading Parish Church, which Jane had attended for almost a year, walking alone across the fields from her cottage home. Weeks turned into months and still Jane was missing, until one day an elderly village woman brought a message telling him that the child was seriously ill and had been asking for him.

Conscience-struck at his neglect, Richmond questioned the woman more closely.

'Sir, I go in most days to speak with her,' she replied, 'and all her talk is about the Bible and Jesus Christ, about life, death, heaven and hell and the books you used to teach her. Her father says he will have no such goings-on in his house, and her mother scoffs at her.'

Enquiring the way to Jane's cottage, Richmond hurried along the country track the following day, still chiding himself for his negligence. At last he found the small thatched home, nestling into the steep hillside, with its wild honeysuckle creeping up the walls. As no one seemed to be about, he pushed open the door and climbed the stairs. But he was unprepared for the sight which greeted him. There lay the sick child, and at her side the old woman who had brought the message. The only furnishing, apart from two dilapidated beds, was a three-legged stool and an old oak chest. The floor was broken and uneven, the walls crumbling and the windows patched with paper. Most startling of all was the change in Jane's appearance. The young face now bore every mark of one terminally ill with tuberculosis.

A bright smile lightened her features as she saw her minister standing at the door. Then with tears streaming down her cheeks Jane said simply, 'I am so glad to see you, sir!'

Sitting down beside her, Richmond asked about her illness, expressing his regret that he had not come before. Then he began to question Jane about her spiritual experience. 'Do you really want to be a true Christian, my dear child?' he began.

'Oh yes!' was the girl's instant reply. 'I want it more than anything else.' The colour rushed to her cheeks as she began to speak of her desires after God and the salvation he offered to sinners.

'What made you think so seriously about the state of your soul?' Richmond enquired next.

'Your talking about the graves in the churchyard and telling us how many young children were buried there,' Jane responded. 'I remember you saying, "Children, where will you be in a hundred years from now?" All the way home and all through that night, these words were in my mind, "Children, where do you think you shall go when you die?" I thought I must leave off my bad ways or where would I go when I died?' Now Richmond realized that behind the apparently dull exterior had been a child earnestly seeking salvation.

'I had been thinking one day,' continued Jane, 'that I was neither fit to live or die; for I could find no comfort in this world, and I was sure I deserved none in the other. On that day you sent me to learn the verse on that headstone, and then I read the one next to it:

> Hail! glorious gospel, heavenly light, whereby
> We live with comfort and with comfort die.

I wished that glorious gospel was mine, that I might live and die with comfort; and it seemed as if I thought it would be so. I never felt so happy in all my life before.'

As he listened, Legh Richmond realized with a rush of joy that here in this dying child was the first convert of his ministry in that place.

Again and again in the following weeks Richmond picked his way along the country track to Jane's cottage. She was growing noticeably weaker, but always he found the same eager spirit, the same longing to speak of eternal things, the same deep sense of sin and love for the Saviour. Realizing that his opportunities to teach this earnest young Christian might soon be over, Legh Richmond decided to turn his visits into times of regular instruction on the privileges and duties of believers.

Each time he called Jane's understanding of spiritual truth seemed to increase. But one day she evidently had something weighing on her mind. The colour crept into her cheeks as she said, 'Sir, there is one thing I want to ask you...' Then she hesitated.

'What is it?' enquired Richmond kindly.

At last with a rush of words she said, 'May a child as young as I am be admitted to the Lord's Supper?'

Knowing her time was short, Richmond agreed that when he had taught her more of the significance of the sacrament, they would commemorate Christ's sufferings and death together at Jane's bedside, and ask the elderly neighbour who had so frequently spoken with Jane to join them.

At his next visit, Richmond was greeted at the door by this friend. 'Perhaps, sir, you will not wake her just yet for she has dropped asleep, and seldom gets much rest, poor girl!' said the neighbour.

Climbing the stairs quietly, Richmond discovered Jane propped up in a half-sitting position, her Bible still open at the narrative of the crucifixion which she had been reading. One outstretched finger marked the verse she had reached — the prayer of the penitent thief: 'Lord, remember me when thou comest into thy kingdom.'

Jane stirred in her sleep, and half woke. 'Lord, remember me... remember me... remember a poor child...' she murmured. Waking fully, she realized she was not alone, and blushed in confusion and embarrassment. 'How long have I been asleep?' she asked. 'Oh sir, I am very sorry.'

But with so fitting an introduction to the things he wish to teach this dying child, Richmond spoke of the penitent heart which alone could qualify a believer to take part in the Lord's Supper.

Richmond did not stay long that day for Jane was very ill. Her fits of coughing and her struggle for breath made it hard for her to concentrate, but the next time the three met in that drab room, with its patched windows and broken furniture the glory of the presence of Christ transformed the comfortless surroundings as three believers commemorated together the sacrifice of Calvary.

'Sir, I shall never forget this day,' said Jane, as Legh Richmond rose to leave.

'Nor I' added her elderly friend. 'Surely the Lord has been in the midst of us three today.'

One concern still weighed heavily on Jane's mind. 'O sir,' she exclaimed to Richmond one day as he visited her yet again. 'I wish you would speak to my father and mother and little brother, for I am afraid they are going on very badly. They drink and swear and quarrel... it does grieve me so, and if I speak a word to them about it, they are angry.'

Jane's mother, who had realized how short were her daughter's remaining days, had not objected to Legh Richmond's visits. But on one previous occasion, when he had been upstairs with Jane, she had arrived back at her house and, unaware of his presence, indulged in a torrent of evil and abusive language. Suddenly realizing she had been overheard, she disappeared out of the back door and seemed to avoid him from that time onwards. Whenever he arrived she appeared to be out.

At last it occurred to Richmond that she could see him coming from the window and was making a hasty exit to escape the rebuke she knew she deserved. Then he decided to approach the cottage from a different direction so that he might have the opportunity of challenging her on her spiritual state. Arriving unnoticed on the next occasion, he paused at the sound of voices from Jane's room. 'Mother, mother,' Jane was saying. 'I have not long to live. But I must, indeed I must say something for your sake before I die. O mother! You have a soul; and what will become of it when you die?'

'Oh dear, I shall lose my child—and what shall I do when you are gone, my Jenny?' sobbed Jane's mother.

Afraid to interrupt, Richmond listened as Jane pleaded with her mother: 'Mother, you must flee to Christ. You must repent and turn from your sin. Do for your own sake, for my sake and for my little brother's sake...' As Jane's strength was fast ebbing, Richmond decided he must make his presence known, but even so he could add little to the child's earnest exhortations.

As he was leaving Jane recovered sufficiently to say faintly, 'Come again soon, sir; my time is very short.'

Early the next morning, while it was still dark, a messenger hammered on the door of the vicarage with an urgent request that he should go immediately to Jane, for her life was fast slipping away and she was asking for him. Legh Richmond hurried once more to the cottage.

Standing at the half-open door, he heard Jane's voice. 'Do you think he will come? I shall be glad—so very glad to see him before I die.'

Quickly mounting the rickety stairs, Richmond stood beside the girl's bed. Unable to speak she gazed at him until at length she said, 'Sir, I am going fast. I was afraid I should never see you again in this world.'

'My child, where is your hope?' enquired Richmond gently. Lifting her finger she pointed first heavenward and then to her own heart and replied, 'Christ there, Christ here.'

Holding out her hands to her mother and father, Jane said simply, 'Think of me when I have gone... remember your souls... O for Christ's sake remember your souls.' Taking her younger brother by the hand, she pleaded: 'Thomas, I beg you to leave off your bad ways... read the Bible... I give you mine... I have found it a precious book.'

Then with one supreme effort she turned to her pastor and said, 'Sir, you have been my best friend on earth—you have taught me the way to heaven, and I love and thank you for it. You have spoken to me of the love of Christ and he has made me to feel it in my heart... I shall see him face to face... He will never leave me nor forsake me...'

Quite suddenly she flung her wasted arms around her minister and declared, 'God bless and reward you... my soul is saved! Christ is everything to me... Sir, we shall meet in heaven, won't we? Oh yes! yes!... Then all will be peace... peace... peace.'

And these were Jane's last words: only a young village girl, but a child who believed—and one of whom this world was not worthy.

Elizabeth Bunyan:
Out of weakness made strong

Elizabeth, second wife of John Bunyan, the tinker of Bedford and author of Pilgrim's Progress, *was probably born around the year 1638, and would therefore have been about twenty years of age when she married Bunyan in 1658. Soon after Charles II's restoration to the throne in 1660, Bunyan was imprisoned for his refusal to attend his local parish church and to refrain from preaching. Elizabeth's support during his twelve years in a Bedford jail marks her out as a woman of outstanding faith and courage.*

When John Bunyan asked Elizabeth to marry him he was inviting her to share, not only his life, but also his sufferings. John's first wife had died the previous year leaving a void in the family circle almost impossible to fill.

Mary, who had married John in the days of his unbelief, had come from a godly home, and though the young couple had 'not so much household stuff as a dish or spoon betwixt us both,' she did possess two religious books which her father had given her. Often she would read to him from these and urge him to reform his ways. She had borne with him in the long years of his spiritual travail as he struggled against doubt and temptation in his search for peace of conscience and reconciliation with God. And during their nine years of marriage four children had been born to John and Mary Bunyan. When she died in 1658 the loss had seemed irreparable, bringing distress to the entire family, even down to 'the least boy,' as Bunyan himself records.

Alone and in need, he had assumed the heavy responsibility of caring for his four motherless children as well as supporting the family financially. But as the months passed it became increasingly clear to him that he must remarry, for his family's sake as well as for his own.

Since the loss of Mary a yet darker shadow had been gathering over John Bunyan's life. The death of Oliver Cromwell in 1658 spelt an end to the period of toleration enjoyed by those men and women who felt unable to conform to the restrictions imposed on their worship by the Church of England. Although no laws had yet appeared on the statute books forbidding all gatherings for worship other than at the parish church, the threat of persecution was real. Already the small group of believers with whom Bunyan was associated had been turned out of their place of worship, St John's in Bedford. Now they had to meet wherever they could, sometimes at the home of one of their members or in some isolated venue—a barn or even a stable. Members had faced crippling fines, and even the confiscation of their tools of trade, for non-attendance at the parish church. After the death of their previous pastor they had been looking increasingly to John Bunyan, whose gifts as a preacher were already apparent. But all John's activities were also being carefully monitored by the local magistrates, for it was widely known that this tinker had the audacity to combine his daily labour with preaching at many secret locations.

John Bunyan's proposal to Elizabeth in the light of all these circumstances, and with his own liberty under constant threat, was indeed an invitation to this young woman to accept a life fraught with hazard and potential suffering. Pondering her decision, Elizabeth would have been well aware of the burden it would place upon her shoulders and of the trials it might bring. Scarcely more than a teenager herself, she would immediately face all the exacting demands of family life. John's eldest child, also called Mary like her mother, would have particular need of her care, for the eight-year-old was blind and far from strong. Elizabeth, the second child, was four, John only two years of age, and baby Thomas little more than a year old. Elizabeth's acceptance of John Bunyan's proposal spoke highly of both the character and faith of this young woman.

Scarcely a year of married life had elapsed before Elizabeth tasted to the full that cup of suffering which her marriage entailed. Charles II had been restored to his father's throne in May 1660, promising 'liberty for tender consciences.' But such promises proved to be only empty words. Six months later a warrant was issued for the arrest of the honest tinker-preacher.

On 12 November 1660, fully aware of the risk they were taking, some forty believers made their way quietly to an isolated farmhouse at Lower Samsell, thirteen miles south of Bedford. Forewarned that their secret location was under surveillance, John Bunyan hesitated before proceeding with the meeting. If he were arrested and thrown into prison, what would happen to Elizabeth, now expecting her first child? And who would provide for his family, for he was their only breadwinner? Thrusting aside such anxieties as unworthy of a man of faith, and realizing how dependent the others were on his example of Christian fortitude, Bunyan opened the meeting. Moments later an ominous rattle at the door confirmed his worst fears. In rushed the local constable, accompanied by the magistrate's servant waving a warrant for the preacher's arrest. John Bunyan was brusquely hurried off to face the local justice of the peace, Francis Wingate.

News of her husband's arrest soon reached Elizabeth. Many accounts circulated amongst the small groups of nonconformists of the atrocities and injustices committed against those who fell into the hands of their persecutors, which could include torture, banishment and even execution. Shock and distress overwhelmed the young woman, bringing on premature labour pains. Eight days later Elizabeth's child was born, but soon died.

Meanwhile days of intense cross-examination followed for Bunyan. Although his unwillingness to attend his local parish church was one cause of offence, far greater was his determination to continue preaching as opportunity arose. Had he but agreed to refrain from this activity, dear to him above all other, he could have purchased his freedom. Try as they might, his interrogators could not extract from Bunyan the assurances they demanded that he would undertake to preach no more.

At last a decision was reached: John Bunyan must remain in prison until the next assizes in two months' time. Then he would face a formal trial. Perhaps two months under prison conditions would prepare him to comply with their demands, and if he still refused he must accept the consequences.

Led away to his cold and cheerless prison, Bunyan was distressed by thoughts of Elizabeth and his family. It seemed that he was destroying all that was dear to him with his own hands, and yet he had no option. 'The parting with my wife and poor children hath oft been to me in this place as the pulling my flesh from my bones,' he wrote as he reflected on the anguish of mind he experienced as he thought of them. They might face hunger and illness, and he could do nothing to help, but it was especially the plight of his blind child, Mary, 'who lay nearer my heart than all I had besides,' that weighed on the prisoner's spirit: 'Oh the thoughts of the hardship my blind one might go under, would break my heart to pieces! "Poor child," thought I, "what sorrow art thou like to have for thy portion in this world? Thou must be beaten, must beg, suffer hunger, cold, nakedness, and a thousand calamities, though I cannot now endure the wind blow upon thee."'

Checking his thoughts that were running to wild extremes, Bunyan added: 'But yet, recalling myself, thought I, "I must venture you all with God though it goeth to the quick to leave you." Oh, I was as a man who was pulling down his house upon the head of his wife and children; yet thought I, "I must do it, I must do it."' Only an unusual consciousness of God's love and favour sustained him through those dark days.

For seven weeks John Bunyan awaited trial in the Bedford County Jail—once situated at the corner of Silver Street and the old High Street. As soon as Elizabeth had recovered from her initial trauma and the sorrow of losing her child, she began to visit him each day with the children.

At last in January 1661 Bunyan was led from his prison to face a panel of five magistrates. Standing in the dock, he listened as the indictment was read out in solemn tones: 'That John Bunyan of the town of Bedford, labourer... hath since such a time devilishly and perniciously abstained from coming to church to hear divine service, and is a common upholder of several unlawful meetings and conventicles to the great disturbance and distraction of the good subjects of this kingdom, contrary to the laws of our sovereign lord the king.'

Backwards and forwards swung the arguments, and always Bunyan had an answer for his accusers. But no scriptural explanations could convince the perverted judgement of the magistrate's bench.

At last they passed sentence. It was all he had anticipated but with an additional ugly twist: 'You must be back to prison again, and there lie for three months following; and at three months' end, if you do not submit to go to church to hear divine service, and leave your preaching, you must be banished from the realm; and if after such a day as shall be appointed you to be gone, you shall be found in this realm... you must stretch by the neck for it, I tell you plainly.'

Distressed at the brutality and injustice of such a verdict, Elizabeth began to think of ways in which she might be able to help her husband. Her first noble endeavour was to travel to London and present a petition for his release to Lord Barkwood, who, according to hearsay, might well be favourable to the plight of nonconformists. An astonishing undertaking for a seventeenth-century country girl, this involved an arduous two or three days of travel with the nights spent at wayside inns.

Arriving at last outside the House of Lords, Elizabeth requested an interview with Lord Barkwood, but it proved futile. He conferred with other members of the Upper House, and together their lordships excused themselves from acting on her behalf by telling Elizabeth that they could not help because such matters were for the judiciary to decide and she must appeal to them at the next assizes.

The king's coronation in April 1661 was accompanied by the release of many felons in order to impress the populace with

Charles II's magnanimity. Prison gates swung open, allowing numerous criminals to walk free, but for the honest tinker of Bedford there was no freedom. His name seemed to be excluded from every list of those who were to be pardoned. No alternative remained for John and Elizabeth Bunyan but to wait for the next assizes.

The Bedford Midsummer Assizes were to be held in August that year and once again Elizabeth was determined to do all in her power to help her husband. If she could submit John's case in person to Sir Matthew Hale, a judge known for his equity and compassion, she felt she might obtain justice. Pressing through the crowds, Elizabeth made her way to the Swan Inn, where four judges were assembled to pass sentence on all cases accumulated since the last assizes. Suppressing her fears, she approached Sir Matthew and presented her petition. The judge received it kindly and, promising to look into the matter, said he would do all he could to help the young woman, but, he added discouragingly, he feared there might be little he could do.

Anxious lest her case should be ignored, Elizabeth, with her husband's encouragement, planned a yet bolder expedient. She waited by the roadside the following day for the coach bearing Judge Hale and Judge Twisdon to the Swan Inn. As it approached she took careful aim and threw her petition in at the open window. Possibly this was an unwise move, for her audacity exasperated Twisdon who snatched up the petition and angrily declared that there could be no liberty for the tinker; he was a convicted person who could not be set at liberty unless he would undertake not to preach again.

Surely if she could only plead with Judge Hale in person there might yet be hope, thought Elizabeth. So on the third day of the assizes Bunyan's courageous wife pressed through the crowds once more and flung herself before Sir Matthew. A good man, Sir Matthew was inclined to listen as Elizabeth insisted that her husband's conviction was unlawful, basing her plea on the fact that Bunyan had been imprisoned for attending a private service of worship before any laws had yet appeared on the statute books making such gatherings illegal. But Judge Chester, one of the magistrates who had heard Bunyan's case at his trial in January, was incensed that his judgement should be brought into question in this way. Stepping up to Sir Matthew, he spoke disparagingly of John Bunyan, describing him as 'a hot-spirited fellow who was lawfully convicted.' Once more she had failed.

All now seemed lost as Elizabeth stepped back miserably into the crowd. But suddenly the high sheriff of the court tapped her on the shoulder. He had watched all that had taken place and kindly suggested that if she could speak to Sir Matthew when the judges were relaxing together after the hearings were concluded, she might have more chance of success in her petition.

Motivated by her love for her husband and her own and the family's need, Elizabeth ventured into the Swan Chamber where all the dignitaries of the town, together with the judges and magistrates, were exchanging pleasantries. Flinging herself before Sir Matthew Hale, she said, 'My Lord, I make bold to come once again to your Lordship, to know what may be done with my husband.' She then explained yet again the grounds of her plea: 'He is kept unlawfully in prison; they clapped him up before there was any indictment against the meetings.'

The sight of the tinker's wife back again infuriated Judge Chester. 'My Lord, he was lawfully convicted,' he insisted as Elizabeth begged again and again for clemency. 'It is recorded, it is recorded,' barked the exasperated judge dogmatically, suggesting that the mere record of the fact put an end to the matter.

'But it is false, it is false,' averred Elizabeth repeatedly, especially when Judge Twisdon also entered the conversation, calling Bunyan a 'breaker of the peace.'

Seeing that no argument would prevail, Elizabeth had only one defence left—her own pitiable condition. Directing her words to Sir Matthew, she said, 'My Lord, I have four small children that cannot help themselves, of which one of them is blind, and have nothing to live upon but the charity of good people.'

'Hast thou four children?' asked Sir Matthew in surprise, as he looked into Elizabeth's girlish face. 'Thou art but a young woman to have four children.'

'My Lord,' replied Elizabeth, 'I am but stepmother to them, having not been married to him yet two full years. Indeed, I was with child when my husband was first apprehended; but being young... I, being dismayed at the news, fell into labour and so continued for eight days, and then was delivered, but my child died.'

'Alas, poor woman,' Hale replied sympathetically, particularly when he heard of the child she had lost. But in spite of all, Elizabeth's pleas were in vain. Realizing that he had no support from other members of the bench, Sir Matthew at last advised her to seek out a writ of error or a personal pardon from the king himself.

At this, Judge Chester snapped angrily, 'My Lord, he will preach and do what he likes.'

'He preaches nothing but the Word of God,' interposed Elizabeth.

'He preaches the Word of God?' snarled Twisdon sarcastically, lunging threateningly towards Elizabeth as if he were about to strike her. 'His doctrine is the doctrine of the devil.'

'My Lord,' responded Elizabeth gallantly, 'when the righteous Judge shall appear it will be known that his doctrine is not the doctrine of devils.'

Clearly honour and truth counted for little in such circumstances, and Elizabeth could see that nothing would be done. No longer able to restrain her tears, she wept as she made her way back through the crowd. But her grief was not for her own situation, nor even for the harsh treatment she had received, but, as she later told her prisoner husband, it was the thought of the 'sad account such poor creatures will have to give at the coming of the Lord, when they shall there answer for all things whatsoever they have done in the body, whether it be good or whether it be bad.'

For twelve long years John Bunyan lay in Bedford jail Elizabeth struggled valiantly to bring up his family on the slender income he received from his writings and from the laces he made and sold at the prison gate. Each day blind Mary brought a jug of soup for her father, but gradually she grew frailer. Day by day the sight of her slender form and drawn features distressed her parents and increased their sense of helplessness. Her death at only sixteen years of age intensified the sufferings endured by John and Elizabeth.

At last in 1672 John Bunyan was released under the terms of the Declaration of Indulgence issued by Charles II. Aged forty-three and with the best years of his manhood spent behind bars, John Bunyan had nevertheless overturned all his antagonists' merciless purposes, for during those years a steady stream of books had flowed from his fertile mind. And these books would be read for generations to come, long after the voice of the preacher they had tried to silence was stilled in death. Gladly the Bedford Meeting appointed him their pastor and, apart from one further short period of imprisonment, the tinker of Bedford spent the remaining sixteen years of his life in the calling he loved above all other as a preacher of the gospel of God's grace. Two children of her own gladdened Elizabeth's later years: Joseph, appropriately named to commemorate her husband's release, who was born in 1672, and his sister Sarah. But always their joys were tempered by the knowledge that renewed persecution could break up the family circle at any moment. The deteriorating political situation posed a constant threat as James II followed his brother Charles to the throne.

Despite a constitution broken by protracted years of imprisonment, John Bunyan spared himself no exertion, either as he toiled at his writing, or as he rode off on some distant preaching engagement. Ever watchful over her husband's health, Elizabeth must have looked with dismay at the darkening storm clouds as John set out once more, first for Reading and from there on to Whitechapel in London, where he was due to preach one Sunday in August 1688.

The threatened storm broke in all its ferocity as Bunyan neared London. Drenched to the skin, he caught a chill and was clearly far from well when he arrived. And although his friends cared for him as best they could, his condition soon turned to pneumonia. The deterioration was so rapid that before a messenger could summon Elizabeth or the children, this Valiant-for-Truth had crossed over the last river. He was just sixty years of age.

For Elizabeth it was a loss indeed, depriving her of a faithful and devoted husband and her children, Joseph and Sarah, of a much-needed father. Financially too she faced yet again days of poverty, for there is evidence that Bunyan had still needed to maintain his secular employment up to the end of his life.

Glancing into his study one day (probably undisturbed since he had ridden off on that sultry morning), Elizabeth noticed many piles of carefully written sheets of paper—works which Bunyan had written but had not published, including one manuscript which still lay unfinished on his desk.

In urgent need of income, Elizabeth placed an advertisement in a newspaper of the time, *Mercurius Reformatus*: 'Mr John Bunyan, Author of the *Pilgrim's Progress* and many other excellent books, that hath found great acceptance, hath left behind him ten manuscripts prepared by himself for the press: his widow is desired to print them...'

A London comb-maker, Charles Doe, already devoted to John Bunyan, saw the advertisement and hurried to Bedford. He quickly agreed to turn publisher and print all of Bunyan's works which Elizabeth could provide. And so the world was given some of Bunyan's most treasured books, including *The Heavenly Footman* and *The Acceptable Sacrifice*.

Only three more years of life remained for Elizabeth herself. In 1691, still in her early fifties, she too, like Christiana in her husband's *Pilgrim's Progress*, came to the verge of the river: 'Now the day drew on that Christiana must be gone. So the road was full of people to see her take her journey. But behold all the banks beyond the River were full of horses and chariots which were come down from above to accompany her through the City Gate... The last word she was heard to say here was, "I come Lord to be with thee and to bless thee.'" Equally Elizabeth Bunyan must have received a triumphant welcome into the Celestial City. And by her fortitude and faith this loyal wife and mother has also earned a well-deserved place among the heroines of the church of Jesus Christ on earth.

Robert Jermain Thomas: A single, steady aim

Korea, known as 'the Hermit Kingdom,' was closed, not only to the gospel, but to all contact with any nation apart from China until 1871. However, there were courageous endeavours to take the gospel to the Korean people before that date, and Jermain Thomas's attempts in 1863 were not without spiritual fruit.

Robert Jermain Thomas and his wife Caroline faced a hazardous future as they contemplated sailing to China as missionaries in 1863. Few had yet set foot in that vast and unknown land in order to bring the gospel of Christ to its teeming peoples. In 1807 Robert Morrison had tried to enter, under the auspices of the London Missionary Society, but could penetrate no further than Canton. Here he carried out his invaluable work of translating the Scriptures, dying in 1834. Representatives of a number of missionary societies had arrived after the Treaty of Nanking had opened up certain coastal towns to Westerners in 1842. But they were widely scattered and their endeavours met with frequent opposition. Hudson Taylor had been in the country for nine years, but he too was still a solitary figure. His vision of twenty-four new missionaries, two for each province, which was to lead to the formation of the China Inland Mission in 1866, lay as yet in the future.

The son of a Welsh Congregational pastor, Jermain, as he was generally called, was born in 1839 in Rhayader in Powys. With his brother and four sisters, the nine-year-old moved to Llanover, near Abergavenny, in 1848 when his father took over the pastoral charge of the Independent church in the town. The boy soon showed a natural flair for languages, excelling at French, Latin and Greek, which he studied at Llandovey College. Later he was to add to his repertoire a number of other European languages.

Jermain's father, described as an 'acceptable, attractive and evangelical preacher,' was delighted when his son spoke of a desire to enter the ministry and gave him all the encouragement he could. This steady purpose dominated Jermain's thinking and soon after his seventeenth birthday he applied to enter New College, London, to begin theological studies. But he was too young. Undeterred, he proposed teaching for a year in Oundle, Northamptonshire, until he was eighteen; after this he applied once more to New College, and this time gained admittance.

During the course of his studies the young man met several other students who spoke of their hopes of sailing to China as missionaries. As they discussed their aspirations and future plans, the desire to give his own life in such service to his God gripped Jermain's imagination. Impetuous by nature, he found the thought of waiting until he had completed his course too hard a discipline to sustain. He applied to the college authorities for permission to cut short his studies and sail with his friends. Not surprisingly, he was told he must wait, a decision he found hard to accept. Leaving the college for a year, he taught privately. But with increasing maturity he began to realize that he had been governed by his natural impetuosity and applied for readmission.

At last, his studies completed, the young Welshman gained further academic accolades as he not only graduated with his BA degree, but was also awarded a coveted prize as the most outstanding student of the year. But despite this, the vision he had caught of bringing the gospel of hope to the darkened land of China still burned brightly in his heart and he lost no time in applying to the London Missionary Society.

In 1858, five years earlier, Britain had concluded a treaty with China, made under duress as the capital, Peking, stood on the brink of capture by British forces. This treaty had secured more favourable conditions for missionaries who wished to enter the country, allowing them to travel inland.

With the prospect unfolding before him of being able to reach many unevangelized peoples, Jermain Thomas preached his first sermon at his father's church after his graduation. He took as his text 'Jesus Christ, the same, yesterday, today and for ever'—words which were to console and strengthen the young man in all the trials that lay ahead. Then without further delay he married Caroline Godfrey, a girl from Oundle in Northamptonshire, whom he had probably met while teaching near her home before he started his training.

Six weeks after Thomas's ordination in June 1863, the young couple embarked for China on the *Polmaine*. Sailing with them was a Scottish missionary, Alexander Williamson, with his wife and child, returning to China, and a single woman missionary candidate. As they left home and family Jermain and Caroline would have been well aware that they might never again see the faces of their loved ones.

A long voyage followed, sailing around the Cape, for the Suez Canal, though under construction, was not yet opened to shipping. Doubtless the prospective missionaries made good use of the time by trying to master the rudiments of the Chinese language and studying Morrison's translation of the Scriptures. During the four-month voyage a deep and enduring bond of friendship was established between Jermain and the older missionary, Alexander Williamson.

Arriving at last in Shanghai in December 1863, Jermain and Caroline faced all the problems of adjusting to a different climate and culture and a primitive way of life. Letters which the new missionary wrote home to his parents have been preserved, and are like a mirror into his mind at this time. Combined with an almost ecstatic joy at having at last reached the land on which all his aspirations and prayers had long been focused, we can also detect a poignant homesickness as he and Caroline longed for familiar faces and kindly friends in the land of their adoption. As the weeks passed, Thomas's correspondence provides a clearer reason for this conflicting reaction.

The London Missionary Society had established a bridgehead for missionary work in Shanghai, and had placed pioneer missionaries William Muirhead and his wife in overall charge. When the Thomases arrived they immediately moved into the same accommodation as the Muirheads. From the outset relationships between the two couples were strained and sharply divergent views over their aims and duties soon became apparent. Thomas felt that the most important thing for him was to master the language, not just the dialect spoken in Shanghai, but also the Mandarin used in Peking, to equip him for future usefulness. He wished to devote the majority of his time to this endeavour. Muirhead, on the other hand, who appears to have handled the younger man in a somewhat dictatorial fashion, found this annoying, expecting Thomas to make the work in Shanghai his priority.

But all this was little in comparison to the sorrows that were awaiting the new missionary. After three months in Shanghai Thomas decided to spend a fortnight in Hankow, two hundred miles further south, to explore the possibility of opening up another front for missionary outreach. A further purpose behind his journey was to secure a healthier environment for Caroline, who was expecting her first child shortly and had found the Shanghai winter detrimental to her health. Jermain had not been gone many days before Caroline received news of the sudden death of a much-loved friend. The shock of this loss brought on a premature labour, quickly followed by the death of Caroline's baby. As soon as this distressing news reached Jermain he set out on his return journey. But although Caroline had made an initial recovery from her miscarriage, two days later infection set in and within twenty-four hours it was clear that she too was dying. Alone, a stranger in a strange land and with her husband absent, Caroline yet had one who stood by her in her extremity and in her lucid moments she spoke of the consolation of the presence of the Saviour. 'Jesus is very precious to me,' were the last words she was heard to articulate.

By the time Jermain arrived back in Shanghai his young wife had already been buried. The news stunned him. 'The event has quite prostrated me; it was so unexpected,' he wrote. The grief was yet harder to bear because he had reason to believe that the breakdown in relationships with the Muirheads had increased Caroline's suffering. How the twenty-four-year-old missionary must have longed for the consolations of home, and of voices speaking a familiar language! Writing to his parents, he confessed, 'My heart is well-nigh broken,' but revealing his tenacity of spirit, he continued, 'I trust to give myself more completely to the noble work on which I have entered, but at present I feel weighed down by deep grief.' Neither was there any privacy for his grief. From dawn to nightfall he was an object of constant curiosity among the Chinese people; everywhere he turned a crowd followed, intrigued at his every movement, for rarely had they seen a white man before. Now he must cast himself anew on the unchanging Christ about whom he had preached.

Six weeks later Thomas wrote from Shanghai to the mission board in London asking to be allowed to work in Hankow. His bereavement and the circumstances surrounding it made him feel the acute need of a fresh start. But permission for such a move was refused. So for a further seven months he continued studying and working in Shanghai. During this time relationships with the Muirheads did not improve.

At last Thomas reached the limit of his endurance and wrote to his society once more, begging for an opportunity to move further inland where he felt the opportunities were wide open for reaching the people. And with this second letter he disclosed that behind his request lay also the problems he was encountering at the mission station. 'I love and respect him [Muirhead],' he wrote, 'but I cannot work with him. I assure you I have wished to do so but I feel I cannot brook the treatment that always has been, and I fear always will be, in store for his colleagues.' But again the society turned down the request. Jermain Thomas promptly resigned from the London Missionary Society.

He was not, however, without friends. Alexander Williamson, working with the National Bible Society of Scotland, had kept in regular touch with the younger missionary and, knowing of his predicament, had found him a secular job in Chefoo, where he himself was based. Chefoo, which was also on the coast, was four hundred miles north of Shanghai, and here Thomas was to work as a customs officer. Such employment would bring him into constant contact with Chinese, Malays, Mongolians and also Koreans, and therefore lead to opportunities to learn both the languages and cultures of these peoples. An additional consolation was, of course, the fellowship and companionship of his older friend.

Jermain Thomas had not been in Chefoo more than six weeks, however, before he began to ponder his hasty resignation. A man of sensitive conscience, he realized that he had acted precipitously. He also wondered if he had misjudged his senior missionary to some degree. So he wrote to the London board of the LMS once more, this time confessing that he had been 'too independent' and asking to be reaccepted. He admitted a change of attitude to Muirhead, saying he both loved and esteemed him, and added, 'If God spares my life I trust that having been thus chastened by him, I may by his grace devote myself steadily and lovingly to his service alone.'

As he awaited a reply from London, Thomas continued working as a customs official, and while employed in this way he met two Koreans, who professed to be Christians. Amazed, he began to speak to them in Chinese, a language with which they were familiar in addition to their own Korean tongue. But as they talked he discovered that all they knew of the Christian religion had come from some Roman Catholic priests who had managed to enter their country in disguise. These men had not even heard of any other form of Christian teaching. Known as the 'Hermit Kingdom,' Korea was a closed land, and had been so for more than six hundred years, not only to the gospel, but to all outside influences from any nation apart from China.

Jermain Thomas also made another discovery: he found that all educated Koreans could read Chinese, for there were remarkable similarities between the two languages. Chinese Bibles could therefore be used in Korea and, in addition, Thomas realized that, with his own linguistic gifts, he would not find it difficult to acquire a working knowledge of Korean. Gradually a new ambition began to formulate in his thinking: why could he not take the gospel to the Korean people? If the Roman Catholic priests had enough courage to risk their lives to propagate their faith, could he not dare to do the same? A short voyage of only four days across the Yellow Sea from Chefoo would bring him to Pyongyang, capital of Korea.

The concept steadily gained momentum in his heart until a new imperative had gripped him: now he knew that he must venture or die in the attempt. Delay seemed intolerable to the zealous missionary. Writing to his mission board, he shared with them his new desire to enter the forbidden land of Korea with the gospel. Possibly anticipating objections, he closed his letter by adding that he trusted that 'the directors will approve of our efforts to spread the doctrine of the Bible unmixed with Romish error in this unknown land.'

Thomas did not act in all this without consulting his fellow missionaries. He first discussed the question with his friend Alexander Williamson, who was prepared not only to fund the endeavour, but agreed to travel down to Peking with him, in company with their two Korean acquaintances. Here they would set their ideas before the other LMS missionaries who were stationed in that city. To Thomas's delight his vision met with approval, and so it was decided that he should sail to the islands west of the Korean mainland accompanied by his Korean guides. Equipped with copies of the Scripture in Chinese and other printed material, he would stay for about three months, during which time he might try to enter the mainland incognito to reconnoitre the possibilities for missionary work. Living among the Koreans in this way, he hoped also to master the language, in order to begin translating the Scriptures into Korean.

So in September 1865, less than two years after his arrival in China, Jermain Thomas sailed in a Chinese junk across the Yellow Sea to Korea, accompanied by his guides. Finding shelter among the villagers in these coastal islands, he began, with his limited

Korean, 'to announce to the poor people some of the most precious truths of the gospel.' Hostile and frightened, most were slow to respond, for they could face death if they were caught accepting foreign goods. But with his dark hair and bronzed features, Thomas managed to avoid detection and his rapidly improving grasp of Korean enabled him to persuade many to accept the Bibles and other literature he had brought.

Convinced of the feasibility of missionary work in Korea, Jermain Thomas returned to Peking overland through the mountainous and bandit-infested land of Mongolia. Gradually he formed plans which seemed feasible in the situation. He might possibly try one more exploratory mission, taking with him a quantity of Bibles and other literature. Buddhism, he had learnt, was on the wane in the country, and many, particularly in the rural areas, had been partially enlightened through the labours of the Catholic priests. The seed of the Word of God might therefore find ready soil in which to grow. After this he purposed to establish his home in the Tadivostok area of Russia, which bordered on north Korea. Here many Korean refugees were to be found and from this vantage-point he would work and wait until the right moment to enter the 'Hermit Kingdom' itself had come. During his recent absence letters had come from London accepting his apology for his hasty resignation and restoring his status as an official representative of the LMS.

However, while Jermain Thomas was in Peking gathering printed materials for his proposed second visit to Korea early in 1866, news began to filter through of a grievous massacre in that country of nine French Roman Catholic priests, who had been secretly at work there, and up to eight thousand of their Korean adherents. Clearly the authorities were deeply hostile to any form of missionary activity. This news cast a dark shadow across Thomas's plans, but at this stage nothing could dampen the zeal of the Welsh missionary to reach the people whose spiritual needs lay so heavily on his heart.

Not long after hearing this appalling report. Thomas learnt of an expedition being organized by the French High Admiral, which planned both to avenge the deaths of these French nationals and also to attempt a rescue of two other priests who were believed to be in hiding. With his grasp of the Korean language, Thomas was persuaded to join the expedition. The eager missionary's desire to reach the Korean people prevailed over his better judgement and he unwisely accepted the invitation. Gathering together all the tracts and Bibles he had accumulated, he travelled back to Chefoo, although in doing so he was acting against the advice of most of his fellow missionaries, in order to await the arrival of the fleet.

But the fleet never came, having been diverted to some other more pressing cause. All ready to venture, Thomas then decided to remain in Chefoo to await a vessel crossing the Yellow Sea. Early in August 1866 an ideal opportunity appeared to present itself. An American trading schooner, the *General Sharman,* was prepared to perform the dangerous undertaking of sailing up the Daedong River to the capital Pyongyang in an attempt to open up commerce with Korea.

Laden with cotton, glass, tin and other goods likely to attract Korean traders, the *General Sharman* also took the precautionary measure of carrying a considerable quantity of arms in view of the volatile political situation in the wake of the massacre. Needing an interpreter to negotiate with the Koreans, the American captain had no difficulty in persuading Thomas to join the crew in that capacity. With four other Westerners and nineteen Malays and Chinese on board, the *General Sharman* set sail. Only after the ship had left Chefoo did a letter arrive for Thomas from the LMS in London strongly advising him against taking so grave a risk.

As the schooner neared Korean waters warnings of her approach were carried to the government. Aware of the threatened assault by the French fleet, the Koreans were alarmed and incensed at the presence of a foreign vessel so close to their shores. Orders were issued that any person seen to be acting suspiciously must be captured and summarily executed.

Unaware of the imminent danger, the *General Sharman* cast anchor off a small island at the mouth of the Daedong River.

Here Jermain Thomas disembarked and spoke to the Koreans he met in their own language, distributing Scriptures to any daring enough to accept them. Then the schooner sailed on, slowly zigzagging its way upstream, through dangerous rapids and past concealed mud-flats.

Again the ship cast anchor and this time Thomas invited some of the gathered crowd to visit him on the ship. Two boys complied, enjoying cakes in his cabin and carrying away books with them, while nine adults, their curiosity overcoming their fears, were persuaded to come on board and accept his literature.

Slowly the General Sharman picked its way along the fifty miles up the river towards Pyongyang, and all the time the agitation and suspicion on the bank were increasing. Three times officials from the towns they passed boarded the vessel and Thomas sought to convince them that the purpose of their expedition was in no way retaliatory for the massacre, nor was he a Roman Catholic, but they even mistook the coin he showed them, with Queen Victoria's head on it, for an image of the Virgin Mary.

Thousands of curious and frightened onlookers crowded to the riverside to watch as the schooner sailed past. Whenever it was near enough to the bank, Thomas threw ashore bundles of Bibles, tracts and portions of Scripture into the crowds. Timid Koreans grabbed the packages and disappeared from view, for news had spread that two of the nine men who had come on board the schooner had already been executed.

At last the schooner was safely past the rapids and within sight of the walled capital. Tension rose to new heights as six crew members climbed into the ship's boat to sail towards Sook-syam, not far from Pyongyang. By now food supplies were running short on the schooner and the object of the crew appears to have been to barter goods for necessary provisions.

Conflicting accounts have survived of the following days of action and reaction. But according to the most reliable records, a Korean boat gave chase and was then captured by the crew of the

General Sharman; the chief of police, who was on board, was taken to the schooner as a hostage, possibly along with others who had been on board the Korean vessel. A search was made of the official's person and papers were found on him detailing plans to murder the entire ship's crew. At this point the captain foolishly confiscated all the man's insignia of office and his papers. Stripped in this way, the chief of police would face discredit and certain execution in normal circumstances.

At this point Jermain Thomas begged to be allowed to negotiate with the governor of Pyongyang to arrange terms for the release of the official. When his intervention was refused the crew of the *General Sharman* bundled the bewildered hostages into the ship's boat and rowed them up river. The frantic Koreans on the shore offered a reward for their return, while one man rowed out in an attempt to rescue his fellow countrymen. His small boat was caught in dangerous rapids and while it was eddying precariously the hostages tried to effect their escape by jumping into it. At least one missed his foothold and was drowned in the swirling waters.

We may only guess at Jermain Thomas's mental anguish as these grievous scenes were being enacted. The crew of the *General Sharman* then opened fire, frightened by the threat of imminent retaliation. The Koreans in turn directed all their fury on the waiting schooner until it was peppered with gunshot and bristled with the arrows sunk into its hull. Intermittent firing continued for the next fortnight, resulting in considerable loss of life both on shore and on the schooner. Alarming rumours were also rife among the Koreans: some said the foreigners were intent on robbing the ancient tombs, and others that they were collecting the eyes of children to use as medicine.

Now seriously short of food, and abandoning all hope of negotiation with the infuriated Koreans, the Americans tried to achieve a hasty withdrawal downstream. Swirling mists enveloped the retreating schooner, making navigation, risky at all times, even more hazardous. Then the *General Sharman* struck a sandbank and became stranded—a helpless target. Tying together a number of small boats, the enraged Koreans packed them with pine brushwood and, when the tide rose, set them alight, allowing them to drift like burning arms towards the schooner.

As the wooden hull of the ship caught ablaze, an inferno of smoke and flames quickly engulfed the schooner. Many years later a Korean recollected his father, an eyewitness of the tragedy, telling him that he recalled seeing through the smoke and the mist a white man standing alone on the deck calling out in a loud voice, 'Jesus, Jesus,' many times over and throwing bundles of books from the burning vessel onto the bank.

The trapped crew were left with no option but to jump overboard and wade towards the shore. Armed with handguns and shooting as they came, the men tried vainly to secure a safe landing. But they were an easy target, and were picked off one at a time as they emerged from the water and were killed with knives, clubs and rifles.

Just one man acted differently. He was not shooting. Rather his arms were filled with strange-looking bundles. As he staggered out of the water, he held out his treasure of the Word of God to the people he had come to serve. A boy of twelve grabbed three Bibles and ran off. Others also picked up the books that Thomas dropped.

Standing over the young Welsh missionary was a Korean soldier, ready to club his victim to death. To his amazement the kneeling man addressed him in Korean and urged him to accept the gift of a book. The stern soldier refused. Still more astonishing, instead of pleading for his life, the white man before him closed his eyes and appeared to be speaking to someone else in a language the soldier did not recognize. Opening his eyes once more, the stranger smiled and again pressed the gift of his book on his murderer. How could he kill a man who behaved in such a way? Then, steeling his heart against pity, the soldier rained down blow after blow on his victim's head. Jermain Thomas died, kneeling on Korean soil—the land for which he had sacrificed all. He was twenty-six years of age.

But his death was not in vain. Stricken by what he had done, the soldier picked up the book he had been offered, carried it home and read it. A woman was deeply affected by words she read in a book she found lying on the bank. The boy who had taken the three Bibles gave them to another soldier who tore out the pages and used them as wallpaper for his home. The boy himself later became a Christian; so did the man who had gone to the rescue of the hostages. Although the Korean officialdom tried to gather up and burn all the literature the dying missionary had brought, eager hands stretched out to grab the books, taking them away to read in secret.

The burning of the *General Sharman* evoked widespread anger in America, leading eventually to war between the two countries. Defeated by America, Korea at last signed a treaty in 1871 opening the country to trade and permitting entrance to foreign nationals. And when missionaries finally arrived, almost twenty years after Jermain Thomas's death, they discovered groups of Christians in the towns along the riverside where he had thrown his packages. In Pyongyang itself a small church had sprung up in the very house which had Bible pages pasted on the walls — and not far from the spot where the charred anchor chains of the *General Sharman* were on display. So the seed of the Word of God which Jermain Thomas had sown in dying had germinated and yielded its harvest in the lives of these Koreans.

Like Thomas's homeland, Korea is a land that has seen powerful revivals. A church born in suffering and marked by prayerfulness has become the fastest-growing church in the world, and perhaps the greatest missionary church of the late twentieth century — an undying tribute to the life and witness of Robert Jermain Thomas.

Lavinia Bartlett:
Spurgeon's 'best deacon'

A member of C. H. Spurgeon's church at New Park Street in London from 1856, and from 1861 in the new Metropolitan Tabernacle, Mrs Bartlett conducted a women's Bible class single-handed from 1859 until her death in 1874. The development of this class, which began with only three teenage girls in attendance, is a story that certainly deserves retelling.

Mingling among the vast throng of worshippers converging on the Surrey Gardens Music Hall to hear the youthful Spurgeon was a middle-aged woman, petite and neatly dressed in black. Lines of suffering marked her face, but the high cheekbones and resolute mouth added a look of courage and determination.

Lavinia Bartlett was a regular member of New Park Street Chapel and, together with the rest of the congregation, she had witnessed the spectacular popularity of the 'boy preacher's' ministry which was attracting hearers from all parts of London and beyond. But now in 1859 Mrs Bartlett stood at a critical juncture in her life. Left a widow at only forty-seven years, with two teenage sons to bring up and in poor health herself, she could scarcely have guessed that she stood poised at the beginning of years of service for her God which would eclipse all she had previously known and would lead Spurgeon to say repeatedly, 'My best deacon is a woman.'

Born in 1806 into a middle-class, well-to-do, but only nominally religious family, Lavinia Hartnell had little encouragement to seek a personal and experiential knowledge of God. Serious and mature beyond her years, she was one of seven children, and early accepted responsibility in the home for her younger brothers and sisters. But how the seed of true religion was planted in her heart, we do not know. Although affiliated to the established church, the family would also occasionally attend a small nonconformist chapel near their home in Beaconsfield, Buckinghamshire, then only a village. Perhaps it was here that Lavinia first learnt to pray, for as she grew up she became known among the villagers as 'the praying girl.'

These were the days of large Sunday Schools, and by the time she was twelve years of age Lavinia had begun to teach a class at the Independent chapel where she was to become a member. Her ability as a communicator was quickly noted and as a young teenager she was given responsibility for the senior class, many of her pupils being older than Lavinia herself. And God blessed her endeavours. One pupil, a girl only two years younger than she, left a tribute in verse to the effectiveness of her testimony:

> If I may hope that I have felt
> The love of God my heart to melt,
> To you I trace it as the means,
> And thank you for your care and pains.

> Yet to Another I would look,
> Who my salvation undertook,
> And came to suffer, bleed and die
> For such a worthless wretch as I...

When Lavinia was only fourteen years of age her father died, plunging the family into immediate financial crisis. With little means of support, her mother clearly needed help and Lavinia decided to open a school for village girls, using the fees she received to supplement the family income. Quickly becoming popular, the school started attracting girls from a wide area around Beaconsfield, and while she was giving her young pupils a basic education, she lost no opportunity to point them to her Saviour.

Lavinia Hartnell's time was now constantly engaged in teaching, both on Sundays and during the week, but still she found time and opportunity for secret prayer, which was assuming an all-important place in her life. An old trunk which her father had brought home from America after his youthful travels stood in Lavinia's room. Covered with the skin of an animal which he had shot, it had gradually acquired special significance in his daughter's life, for against that old trunk she had knelt to pray from her childhood days. Many had been the pleas and tears that had ascended to heaven from that spot—for her brothers and sisters, her Sunday School class or her pupils.

And now, as her reputation as 'the praying girl' began to change to that of 'the praying woman,' frequent requests for her prayers and counsel came from villagers, most of whom had little understanding of true religion. Whenever a villager was in trouble, instead of 'Send for the parson' it would be 'Send for the praying woman' and often Lavinia could be found picking her way through the darkness to some lonely cottage in response to a call for help. Not only the respectable and God-fearing sent for Lavinia when they were in distress, but she could also be found kneeling beside some hopeless girl who had sold herself to prostitution, or be summoned by a broken-hearted wife to the deathbed of a drunkard.

As Lavinia Hartnell entered her adult years her school began to alter in character. Reluctant to leave her, young women were wishing to remain at 'school,' and so Lavinia started to teach them a type of embroidery relatively unknown at the time. As her pupils acquired proficiency, they created beautiful clothing and other items decorated with satin-stitch work. Then Lavinia conceived the plan of turning her school into a business and providing employment for these women. Travelling alone to the City of London warehouses with specimens of the work her school could produce, Lavinia cast herself on God for direction and help. Showing remarkable initiative for a young woman in Victorian times, she made contact with some large wholesale warehouse managers, who admired her samples and readily placed orders for the embroidery. One was even prepared to advance capital to set her up in business. Before long, Lavinia was providing employment for over two hundred women and girls.

But a change was at hand. In 1836, at the age of thirty, Lavinia married, now becoming Lavinia Bartlett, and moved to London to be with her husband. One item of furniture could not be left behind, and the old trunk soon joined its owner in her new London home. Two sons were born to Lavinia and her husband in quick succession. Years later Edward, her elder son, was to write of that trunk: 'I shall never forget the spot where our prayers were offered. We two boys knelt by our mother's side at the old trunk, where she had taught her brothers and sisters to pray many years before. She loved that old trunk and we loved it too; for indeed it was an altar unto the living God.'

Soon after her marriage Lavinia Bartlett experienced a serious setback in her health. A heart complaint from which she had suffered since her early years now worsened, leaving her a virtual invalid at times. Unable on some occasions even to join in public worship, she would just sit in the vestry, happy at least to be near the Lord's people. All forms of Christian service now had to be laid aside—a hard discipline for one whose chief joy it had been to exhort others to seek the Lord. But God had a hidden purpose in these years of relative inactivity. For during this period Mrs Bartlett gave herself to prayer in a yet more intense and fervent manner. Her two sons became her mission-field, and their salvation the increasing burden of her life.

Further distress lay in store for the family, for in 1853 a virulent epidemic of cholera swept through London, leaving Mrs Bartlett a widow and her sons fatherless at the ages of fifteen and seventeen. Increasingly frail herself, Lavinia Bartlett prayed yet more urgently for her boys, fearing that her own time might be short. But God's answer to her supplications came from an unexpected source.

The year after her husband's death Mrs Bartlett was surprised, but not impressed, by rumours of a nineteen-year-old boy preacher who had come to nearby New Park Street Chapel. Mere sensationalism and ranting was the opinion she expressed of the young C. H. Spurgeon's preaching when she heard of the crowds that were now filling the Exeter Hall to hear him.

But despite his mother's views, Edward, with all the curiosity of youth, was determined to listen to this preacher, who was only a year older than he was. Deeply moved by all he heard, Edward resolved to return the following Sunday to listen again, and was soon brought to real and personal faith. No longer could his mother resist his appeals for her to accompany him, and as soon as Mrs Bartlett heard the young man pleading with God in prayer, she too knew that here was a ministry she must sit under. Her cup of blessing overflowed when her younger son, George, who had withstood all his mother's ardent exhortations, was also converted under the young Spurgeon's ministry. And the following year the whole family, united in grace, became members of New Park Street Chapel.

With these joys and some improvement in her health, Mrs Bartlett began to wonder whether God yet had any service which she could fulfil. She had not long to wait. In June 1859 she was asked if she could step in at short notice to teach a Sunday School class instead of the regular teacher who had to be away for a month. Hesitantly she accepted, but stipulated that it should not be for any longer than the month, fearing lest it should adversely affect her health.

On her arrival at the church on the first Sunday afternoon, great was her consternation when the person in charge of the Sunday School asked her to take the senior Bible Class instead of the class for which she had prepared. Agreeing only after some persuasion, she discovered just three teenage girls present that afternoon. But by the end of the month those numbers had increased to fourteen and Mrs Bartlett was asked if she would consider continuing to teach the class on a permanent basis. 'If the Lord has given me strength for one month's labour, he will be sure to give me strength for another month,' was her characteristic reply.

So began 'Mrs Bartlett's Class'—an institution which was to grow to legendary proportions in the next fifteen years. Though clearly a woman of remarkable natural abilities, her primary qualification for such a work lay in her passionate desire for the salvation of others and her implicit faith in the promises and power of God. As numbers seeking admission to the class began to climb, space became the most acute problem. An empty building next to the chapel provided a temporary solution, but soon that room was filled to overflowing and young women were seated from the top to the bottom of the adjoining staircase.

What could be done now? The magnificent new Metropolitan Tabernacle was nearing completion and Mrs Bartlett was promised a room in the building for her burgeoning class. But she could not wait. With characteristic determination she led her numerous class to the unfinished Tabernacle and taught them in the upper gallery. And still the numbers grew: fifty increased to eighty, and as the attendance climbed, a spirit of earnest prayer gripped the class which had caught its leader's vision for reaching the unchurched women and girls of London.

Not surprisingly, therefore, the numbers continued to multiply. Eighty became one hundred, which in turn swelled to three hundred. Completed in 1861, the Tabernacle now supplied larger facilities for the class. But as members invited their friends to join, the problem of space became crucial once more as between four and five hundred women crammed into the available accommodation each Sunday. The only room in the Tabernacle large enough to hold such numbers was the Lecture Room currently being used by the main Sunday School. Mrs Bartlett's vision and enthusiasm were irresistible and soon a reluctant Sunday School superintendent was persuaded to evacuate the Lecture Room. In 1865, six years after her tenuous acceptance of the responsibility, between seven and eight hundred women were meeting each Sunday afternoon at the Tabernacle. They ranged from girls in their late teens to grandmothers of seventy years or more and constituted the largest adult class in the world at that time.

Mrs Bartlett led her 'class' single-handed, always addressing them herself. Gifted as a speaker, her messages were more in the nature of exhortations, for she insisted she was not preaching. In these exhortations, grounded on the great doctrinal truths of the faith, she urged Christian women to deeper devotion to Christ and to constant vigilance against sin. Looking on into the future, she would speak with anticipation of the joys laid up in heaven for those who persevered to the end. With tenderness and yet boldness, she pointed out those sins to which most women are particularly prone. And always there was a note of urgency in her messages, for she regarded herself as 'a dying woman,' and feared lest her opportunities to exhort and encourage her class should be cut short at any moment.

But it was in her appeals to the unconverted that Mrs Bartlett's words took on an eloquence born of earnest desire. 'Can you perish? Will you perish, my sister?' she would enquire feelingly. One young woman who happened to enter the room as Mrs Bartlett spoke those very words was converted on the spot. A hearer once transcribed one of these moving addresses and we may even now catch the urgency and pathos of her entreaties:

> There are unconverted ones here. Sinner! Sinner! If you were called to die—what then? Where's your refuge? Have you any? Have you any? Oh! It is a solemn time with some of you. Have you any refuge? 'No,' you say. You have no refuge from the hand of death. Have you any refuge beyond that? You must stand before God as a naked sinner. Oh, is it possible that any of this class should ever perish?... Oh sister, think, think, I beseech you. You hear me now, but you may never hear me again... It is only a thread that keeps you here. There is a storm coming on, the storm of the wrath of Almighty God, which it will be impossible for you to stem or escape. Will you go to bed tonight and be careless of the wrath of God? Can you sleep? I beseech you cry to God where you are sitting; now, on those benches, cry, 'Lord, save me or I perish!' It is from love to your soul that I thus speak, for I know it must live for ever; and dying as you are, I know it must be lost for ever. Can you bear it? Can you bear it? I am going to heaven—will you go with me? Perhaps you say to me, 'I am such a

great sinner.' Ah, my sister, but the blood of Jesus
Christ cleanseth from all sin... I have wept over you
with a heart full of sorrow—go to him, I entreat you.

Not surprisingly, many conversions took place among those who
attended this class, and even among those who came either out of
curiosity or from unworthy motives. When six prostitutes arrived
intending to disrupt proceedings, four were convicted of their
sinful way of life and converted that very day, one of whom
subsequently devoted her life to missionary work.

On another occasion an actress who had been persuaded to
attend against her will left seemingly unimpressed. But she was
back the following week. On the third visit she became convicted
of her sins and as Mrs Bartlett addressed the class she cried out in
despair, 'Lost! Lost! Lost!' Kneeling in prayer later with Mrs
Bartlett, this young woman received an assurance of God's
forgiveness.

An elderly woman who had hardened her mind against all
Spurgeon's earnest gospel appeals for more than two years entered
the room as Mrs Bartlett was speaking. 'Flee from the wrath to
come, sister, flee from the wrath to come,' the class leader was
pleading. The words led to her instant conversion.

So great was the impact of the class each Sunday afternoon
that Mrs Bartlett gave up all her time and energies to it. On a
Tuesday night and again on a Friday the class would gather for
prayer and study of the Scriptures. Numerous money-raising
projects were organized to support the Pastor's College and every
six months these women, many in straitened circumstances
themselves, presented Spurgeon with a generous cheque worth
over five thousand pounds in today's values.

Often in pain, Mrs Bartlett found such service costly, but
refused to heed those who cautioned her to take more rest.
Medical advice likewise went ignored until a serious relapse would
compel her to take time to recuperate. Selecting an isolated
country village where she could rest without being recognized, she
would spend a few weeks away from London, perhaps with her

sons or a friend. But however careful she was, it seemed inevitable that someone would notice her.

Near Margate in 1873 her retreat was discovered and urgent requests came flowing in to address various gatherings of women. Unwilling to allow an opportunity to pass, Mrs Bartlett set out to walk into Margate one Sunday afternoon. She had not gone far before she was overcome by dizziness, a symptom of the condition which had troubled her all her life. Reeling unsteadily, she struggled on, hardly knowing how to remain upright. Just at that moment a woman looked out of her window, and saw the figure in the road below, obviously in some distress. 'There is a lady coming along appearing very ill,' this woman exclaimed to her sister. The sister joined her at the window. 'Why, it's dear Mrs Bartlett of London!' she exclaimed. Quickly the sisters ran to Lavinia's assistance, and asked her into the house to rest while a message was carried to the gathering who had been awaiting her arrival.

The house into which the sick woman had been invited turned out to be a girls' boarding school, and as soon as her strength had returned, the sisters persuaded Mrs Bartlett to address the girls. With typical disregard for herself, she agreed, and the blessing of God came upon that gathering to a marked degree. More than this, the husband of one of the sisters, who was ostensibly a backslider, listened to his visitor's message from the back of the room. Then he knew that he had never before experienced the power of vital religion, and that day marked his true conversion to God.

A woman of intense force of character, Mrs Bartlett refused to allow weakness or pain to rob her of any more opportunities of meeting with her class than was absolutely necessary. And so she toiled on, her all-consuming object to win souls for Jesus Christ. Her one-month trial period with the senior Bible Class had turned to fifteen years before her work was done. Apart from the many women influenced who did not become members of the Tabernacle, or who joined other churches, it was estimated that over one thousand had been converted and had joined the church as a direct result of her endeavours. 'Few could resist the passionate utterances of this Bible teacher,' wrote a friend. 'Such earnestness, coupled with unwavering faith in God's Word, could hardly fail to bring down heaven's blessings. If you ask me the secret of this good woman's success I reply that it lies in her implicit reliance upon God's promises and a strong assurance that he will do all that she believingly asks of him.'

Many who heard of Mrs Bartlett's work wrote asking her how they might achieve similar results. Perhaps her pastor, C. H. Spurgeon, was nearest the mark when he said, 'Love was the secret of her power. Tears flowed from many eyes when she pleaded because her soul was stirred within her. Sometimes the pathos of her addresses was overwhelming.' And the secret of such love was the one she had learnt beside the old trunk. So Spurgeon continues: 'Before they professed faith in Jesus she would pray for them and pray with them, and after conversion she watched over them as a mother over her babe, and trembled lest by any means they should be turned aside by the error of the wicked.' Her home, which Spurgeon fittingly called a 'house of mercy,' was always open to women in spiritual distress. They saw in Mrs Bartlett a true friend and one who cared intensely for their needs and sorrows. Women confided freely in her and many were those who could tell how God had met them as they sat weeping on Mrs Bartlett's settee.

And so in 1875, at the age of sixty-nine, God called this noble and dedicated woman home. On her last Sunday with her class, before she was taken ill on the following Tuesday, she spoke on John 3:3 with unusual urgency, still pleading with the unconverted to seek salvation. Sinking rapidly during that week, Lavinia Bartlett longed to be with her class. 'Take me, oh take me, my dear child, to my dear people' she pleaded with her son. But realizing this was impossible, she continued to pray for them in her lucid moments. 'Lord, save her now, save her now,' she would whisper.

As with most dying believers, her thoughts turned back to the centralities of her faith and the foundation of her confidence before God. Conscious of her sins, she could be heard quoting softly to herself such hymns as:

A guilty, weak and helpless worm,
On thy kind arms I fall;
Be thou my strength and righteousness,
My Jesus and my all.

And before losing consciousness just six days after being taken ill, she was heard to say quietly, 'Jesus, Jesus, Jesus, now take me to thy banqueting house.' By the following morning Lavinia Bartlett had indeed joined that marriage supper of the Lamb.

'My best deacon is a woman,' Spurgeon used to say, and as he addressed her grieving class, he spoke of the effectiveness of the leader they had lost: 'Her unstaggering reliance upon the Saviour has led many of you to confide in him... I do not believe that any mother knew her children better than she knew the members of this class ... her heart was large and her efforts incessant. The loss to us is gain to her. We are thankful of the loan we had of such a woman.'

And Lavinia Bartlett still deserves to be remembered by the Christian church. Words on her gravestone, chosen by Spurgeon, continue to bear silent witness to her worth: 'She was indeed a mother in Israel. Often did she say, "Keep near the cross, my sister."'

Leonard Dober:
A volunteer slave

A member of the Moravian Brethren, Leonard Dober was among the refugees of a persecution in his homeland who fled to Germany in 1722 and found asylum on Count Zinzendorf's territory at Herrnhut. Here the Moravians lived and worked as a community, becoming some of the earliest European missionaries. They travelled to countries as far-flung as Greenland, South Africa and the West Indies.

Leonard Dober could not sleep that night. As he tossed back and forth on his bed he struggled ineffectually to banish from his mind an urgent appeal he had heard that evening from Count Zinzendorf, a man whose word was law among the Moravian Brethren at Herrnhut. The count had just returned from Denmark where he had been paying his respects to the new king, Christian VI, on the occasion of his coronation. There in the court he had met a slave from the West Indies who had entreated him to send someone to his home island of St Thomas to bring the knowledge of Christ to his people, who were destitute of spiritual light and sunk in misery.

Zinzendorf had questioned the man, whose name was Antony Ulrich, more closely about the situation. Yes, he assured the count, warming to his theme, his people's need was desperate. Before he had been taken from his home to Copenhagen in the service of a Danish nobleman, he had often knelt alone on the shore praying for spiritual light and understanding. With his own quest fulfilled as he learnt of Christ while working as a slave in the nobleman's house, Antony frequently thought of the plight of his fellow countrymen and especially of his own brother Abraham and his sister Anna, whose hearts also thirsted after a knowledge of the true God. As they toiled day after day in the relentless heat of the sugar plantations they too longed to hear of one who could transform their lives of misery. Often Antony would pray that some missionary might go to them, but no messenger of Christ had ever yet ventured to those distant shores. For, added the West Indian slave darkly, the personal sacrifice involved in such a mission would be high indeed. Whoever embarked upon it must first of all sell himself into slavery and share the lot of the slaves if he hoped to gain an entry to the island and win a hearing among the people.

Fired with zeal at the prospect of such an opportunity, the count invited Ulrich to visit his Moravian settlement at Herrnhut in person and present his appeal to the young men who lived and worked there. Meanwhile Zinzendorf himself hurried back to Herrnhut to prepare the Moravians for such a challenge. This, he thought, was the very moment for which he had been waiting, for the plight of the unevangelized peoples of the world had long weighed on his mind.

Leonard Dober was among the group of men who had listened enthralled as Zinzendorf shared all he had heard with them. Elated, on the one hand, at the potential for serving their God in so signal a way, the Moravians were yet horrified at the appalling cost entailed in such a mission and shrank from the thought. So now, as Dober wrestled with these issues that night, he found sleep impossible. Surely there was nothing he could do to help the slaves of St Thomas. After all, he was only eighteen years of age and the Moravian Brethren at Herrnhut, among whom he lived and worked, would never place enough confidence in him to allow him to travel so far on such a hazardous commission. And the thought of slavery terrified him. How could he endure such suffering? He could almost hear the merciless crack of the slave manager's whip, the piteous cries of men and women as they stumbled and fell under its remorseless lashes. He anticipated the toil and the heat of the sugar plantations, the filthy conditions and, above all, the degradation of slavery. No, the price was too high. But had not his Saviour bowed before the lash of a Roman whip for the sake of sinners? And could he not contemplate becoming the bond-slave of such a Master?

The night hours crept by and still the scenes refused to fade. Perhaps this was indeed God's voice calling him to sacrifice his life in this way. How could he distinguish between his fancy and the will of God? If only there were someone with whom he could share his thoughts! At last the long night ended and the morning's activities began. But throughout the day his spirit was oppressed and troubled as he thought of the condition of the West Indian slaves.

As soon as his duties as a potter for the Herrnhut settlement were completed, he sought out his friend Tobias Leupold. As the two men sauntered together in the woodland, Leonard confided his desires and apprehensions. To his astonishment he discovered that Tobias had been wrestling with the selfsame burden, had endured the same mental crisis. He also had been anxiously awaiting an opportunity to talk it over with his friend. Together the two young men knelt in the quiet woods, consecrated themselves afresh to God's service and together determined to heed the call of God regardless of personal sacrifice.

In 1722 these settlers on Count Zinzendorf's property in Saxony had fled there from a persecution that had nearly crushed the church of the Moravian Brethren. For more than three hundred years before that date, and predating the Reformation by more than fifty years, little groups of Moravian Christians had clung to gospel truths through ever-changing circumstances—sometimes prospering, at others almost decimated. And now, owing to Count Zinzendorf's generosity, a remnant of this faithful band had found sanctuary in Herrnhut. Here they had lived for ten years prior to Leonard's sleepless night. Full of spiritual zeal, many among them had caught Count Zinzendorf's vision and were contemplating opportunities to spread the gospel of Christ to distant parts of the earth—the first Christian church to undertake such an endeavour—and this was sixty years before William Carey sailed for India.

Following their prayer in the woods, Leonard Dober and his friend rejoined their fellow workers who were returning together to their living accommodation after completing their assignments for the day. As they were passing Zinzendorf's house, Dober overheard a snatch of conversation between the count and a friend: 'Sir, among these young men there are missionaries to St Thomas, Greenland, Lapland and many other countries,' the count was saying. That was enough for Leonard, who took the words as confirmation of his secret thoughts. Without delay he and Leupold wrote to the count offering their services for far-off St Thomas.

To their astonishment, his response was muted, but he agreed to read the letter aloud to the rest of the community, only withholding the identity of the writers. When Count Zinzendorf shared the contents of the letter with the other Moravians, they too reacted negatively. It was a reckless undertaking, declared some; a bid for kudos and glory, added others; while those who had guessed the names of the writers dismissed their courageous offer as delusion, fantasy and attention-seeking.

A full year elapsed without any further action being taken, and still the intolerable condition of the West Indian slaves weighed on Leonard's mind. Unswerving in his intent to become a slave for Christ's sake, Dober dared not allow the issue to remain unresolved. At last Tobias and he decided to write directly to the leaders of the congregation offering their services for this pressing need. This time their offer was taken seriously by their fellow settlers, but the count still doubted if these two young men were God's chosen instruments for so formidable an undertaking. And again no conclusion could be reached.

The only way around the impasse appeared to be by means of an expedient Count Zinzendorf favoured in such cases of indecision. They would cast lots for guidance. A solemn meeting was held and a box known as the Watch Word Box was brought in. This contained numerous pieces of paper on which texts were written. With deep trepidation Leonard drew out a small scrap of paper. Unfolding it he read the words: 'Let the lad go, for the

Lord is with him.' To his grief, when his friend drew his lot, the answer was negative. Tobias was not to join him. Instead an older man, David Nitschmann, was chosen to accompany Leonard until he had settled into his new work.

Before dawn on 21 August 1732 two strange-looking figures could be seen waiting outside Count Zinzendorf's home. Dressed in brown coats, with quaint three-cornered hats, bundles on their backs and a little money for food in their pockets, Leonard Dober and David Nitschmann were ready to begin their long journey to bring the gospel to the needy slaves of the West Indies. The count, who had been spending the night in prayer for their endeavour, drove them in his carriage as far as the nearest town, from where they planned to walk to Copenhagen. The only instruction he gave was to 'Do all in the spirit of Jesus Christ.' Praying over them, the good man sent Dober and Nitschmann on their way.

So was born the Moravian missionary movement, precursor of a work which would take the message of the grace of God worldwide, and herald that great advance of the church of Jesus Christ into the farthest parts of the earth towards the end of the century.

For six hundred miles the two men trudged along the dusty roads; their money soon gone, they were dependent on the kindness of fellow travellers and farmers for their sustenance. At last Copenhagen was in sight. Here they hoped to gain favour at court through their connections with Count Zinzendorf and be granted passage on a ship bound for the West Indies by the Danish West Indian Company.

Far different was the reception they were given. Mockery and incredulity met them at every hand. Had they proposed to travel as ambassadors of some state, it would have been different, but as servants of Jesus Christ, with no other commission than to preach the gospel, they were regarded as a pair of fools. They were asked how they expected to live when they reached their destination. When it was learned that one of the missionaries planned to sell himself into slavery, the derision reached new heights. That would be impossible, they were informed. How could he countenance such degradation? Did he imagine that a white man would even be accepted as a slave?

With patience and persistence Dober and Nitschmann slowly won the favour of some in the royal household. The queen was impressed with their sincerity; her daughter Princess Amalie slipped a few gold coins and a Dutch Bible into Leonard's hand; while the court physician supplied them with a sharp knife for conducting a little basic surgery, should the need arise. At last even the court chaplain espoused their cause and soon a passage to St Thomas, one of the Virgin Islands of the West Indies, was granted. Dober and Nitschmann now embarked on their voyage, far off from all they had known and for Leonard into a life fraught with potential suffering.

For nine weeks they were tossed about on a stormy ocean as they crossed the Atlantic until at last the yellowing rocks and low, green hills of St Thomas came into view. Gazing at their prospective mission-field, scene of torment and sorrow for those they had come to serve—a prospect far different from that which greets the modern tourist—the two men sought out the consolations of the Word of God to strengthen their resolve. The Watch Word box was consulted. 'The Lord of hosts mustereth the host to the battle,' they read on their chosen slip of paper. And surely that same God would not fail them now.

In the event God did not require the costly sacrifice Leonard Dober was prepared to make; his offer of himself as a slave was rejected. Instead both men were hired as servants in the home of the governor of the island. After three months on the island, having assured himself that his young companion could manage alone, Nitschmann relinquished his post and sailed back to Europe. Not long afterwards Dober also requested release from his position in the governor's house, fearing that his situation there was so superior to the lot of the men and women whom he had come to serve that it was an obstacle to his usefulness. Instead he chose to live in a small mud hut on one of the plantations.

No dramatic results attended his testimony, but gradually the people grew to love and trust the young man who would willingly have embraced slavery that they might become free men in Christ. Slowly, darkened minds began to bow before the gospel of God's pity and grace, the brother and sister of the slave who had originally appealed for help, Abraham and Anna Ulrich, being among the first to be touched. When Leonard Dober was recalled by his church four years later for service elsewhere, he had seen the early converts of an amazing work of God which was to expand to thirteen thousand new believers in the West Indian islands before any other missionary society reached those distant shores.

Martha Nelson:
The cause is God's

Born in 1705, Martha was the wife of John Nelson, one of the early converts of John Wesley's ministry in 1738. Together with Benjamin Ingham and William Grimshaw, Nelson was a pioneer preacher in Yorkshire during the Evangelical Revival in the eighteenth century. Not only the preachers, but also their wives and the converts of their preaching would often be the target for physical abuse and persecution from the unruly mobs, frequently incited to violence by the antagonism of local clergy.

Toiling at his work as a stonemason, chipping and shaping stones for a new building, John Nelson one day caught sight of a young woman whom he had never met before. Instantly he resolved that she should be his future wife. For some time the nineteen-year-old had been praying that he might be given a companion in life with whom he could live in a way that would bring glory to God. When he set his eyes on Martha, although he did not even know her name, he felt a sudden confidence that this girl was God's answer to his prayers.

And so, not long after, John and Martha were married. But despite his noble aspirations, John was still a stranger to the grace of God, and so was Martha. John's concern to please God arose out of a profound dissatisfaction with his own way of life which had tormented him since childhood. But to whom could he turn for help? He knew of no one able to answer his problems, for in the early decades of the eighteenth century the people of Birstall, in Yorkshire, where John and Martha Nelson lived, were in spiritual darkness and steeped in superstition. Restless and troubled, John eventually decided to go to London, where he hoped he might resolve his inward crisis. There he and Martha lived for some years and there two children were born to them.

But gradually Martha's health began to deteriorate and so John decided that she and the children should return home to Yorkshire, and he himself would follow shortly. This he did, but back in Birstall, near Leeds, John continued to find himself yet more restless. Day by day as he toiled at his stonemasonry, quarrying and shaping stones, his mind became increasingly perplexed and disturbed about the great issues of life and death, issues beyond Martha's understanding. Why had he been born at all? How could he face the final judgement of God? If only he had been born a sheep or a cow! More than this, strange dreams began to distress him until he announced to Martha that he must return to London, this time on his own. Perhaps he would be able to find the answers he so earnestly sought.

Two years had passed since then and now, early in 1742, John had written to say he was coming home. The intervening months of separation had been hard for Martha. Although John had written regularly and sent his earnings to support the family, she had missed him sorely. Their young daughter had sickened and died, and their little son's life too had hung in the balance. In addition Martha's own fall from a horse had left her with a long-term injury. So John's decision to return was a consolation. But certain comments in his letters also made her wary. Evidently he had been listening to some strange new preaching from a clergyman named George Whitefield who had been banished from the pulpits of the capital and had taken to addressing vast crowds on the commons at Moorfields and Kennington. This, together with the preaching of a certain John Wesley, had apparently affected him profoundly.

So Martha awaited her husband's return from London with mixed feelings. But nothing could have prepared her for the shock she experienced when John arrived. Alight with an inner peace, he declared that he now knew for certain that his sins were forgiven —a strange concept indeed for those days. Worse was to follow for Martha. John began to reprove the neighbours for their sins and urge them also to seek God's forgiveness.

Even John's mother did not escape her son's reproofs. 'Your head is turned,' she commented tartly.

'Yes, and my heart too, I thank the Lord,' was John's ready reply.

Martha was acutely embarrassed at her husband's activities, fearing even to venture out of doors lest she should face the calumny of the neighbours. If only John had stayed in London, she found herself wishing. Unless he could stop upsetting everyone, Martha declared, she would have to leave him, for she felt she could stand the strain no longer. Nor did she escape his exhortations either, although John pointed out that it was his love for her which motivated him to speak in that way. Then Martha's patience finally snapped. 'My happiness with you is over,' she cried, 'for according to you I am a child of the devil and you are a child of God!'

'No,' John replied, 'if you seek redemption in the blood of Christ, we shall be ten times happier than ever.'

Martha only wept. 'I cannot live with you,' she protested.

But John Nelson mingled his rebukes and exhortations with earnest prayer for his family and neighbours. Within weeks of his arrival home seventeen had professed conversion. At last Martha too began to grow concerned for her soul. Now she realized that John's warnings were true. She must either experience the same forgiveness of her sins or perish. Then illness struck, and as her spiritual distress increased, her condition seemed to deteriorate. John watched over her anxiously as her state worsened and her life itself seemed threatened. And all the time he continued to give himself to prayer and fasting for her.

One evening he was reading the Scriptures aloud to a group of neighbours, while Martha lay in an adjacent room, though still within earshot. As she listened, the words struck home to her heart. Then terror seized her, for she recognized she was in imminent spiritual danger. She could feel herself already dropping into a deep abyss—the abyss of the judgement of God against sin. But just as she sensed herself falling, she became conscious of arms stretched out to catch her. Then she heard the merciful words: 'Thy sins are forgiven thee,' and knew that the one who had intervened to save her was none other than the Lord Jesus Christ. At that moment Martha realized that she too had experienced that same pardoning love of God which had brought liberty to her husband.

'My dear,' she exclaimed when John came to her bedside, 'the Lord has healed me both in body and in soul.' Matching her words with actions, Martha rose from the couch, adding, 'I will get up, and praise his holy name!' Writing an account of these things many years later, John recorded, 'From that hour her fever ceased and her heart was filled with praise to God.' Never again did Martha complain of John's activities: she was now a new woman, always supporting her evangelist husband, no matter how high the price, however painful the suffering.

News of Nelson's activities spread rapidly around the closely-knit community. Changed lives incited strong reactions, and everywhere he went the crowds gathered; most came to hear him preach, but some to insult and molest. All day he would labour at his stonemason's work to support the family, for Martha was now expecting another child. In the evening, not waiting for a meal, and still clad in his stonemason's apron, with a chisel slung at his waist, he would hurry to some appointed place where the crowds were already awaiting him. Throughout the benighted villages and towns of eighteenth-century west Yorkshire this earnest stonemason-preacher proclaimed the message of forgiveness of sins through faith in Christ.

But the days were rough and violent, and the mobs were easily incited to abuse the brave preacher. Many were the providences of God delivering Nelson from those intent on harming him. Martha faithfully supported him whenever she was able, standing by him as he preached in the villages and towns around Birstall. But the year after her conversion she too had to endure a baptism of suffering. On this occasion, with her pregnancy far advanced, she had been at Wakefield where the crowds had become particularly vicious. Martha and a few other women turned to go home, a journey of some few miles. But as they were nearing Birstall a group of callous and evil women who had been following them turned on the young mother. 'You are Nelson's wife,' they cried, 'and here you shall die.' Beating and kicking her mercilessly, they killed her unborn child. When John returned from preaching in another place where he himself had narrowly escaped serious injury, he discovered to his sorrow that Martha had lost her baby and was herself so injured that she never fully recovered her former strength. But, he commented, 'God more than made it up to her by filling her with peace and love.'

John and Martha Nelson's trials were only beginning. In May 1744 the vicar of Birstall, anxious to remove such a troublemaker from his area, arranged to have the honest preacher press-ganged for the army on the pretext that he was an idle good-for-nothing. Marched from Halifax to Bradford, Nelson was thrown into a stinking dungeon below an abattoir and was refused even a drink of water to alleviate his thirst. Blood and filth seeped through the boards above, leaving him with nowhere to sit. 'But,' he later wrote in his journal, 'my soul was so filled with the love of God that it was a paradise to me.'

Word of John's plight soon reached Martha, and though she was once again expecting a child, she rose that same night and walked the seven or more miles to Bradford, bringing a little food and drink. At four in the morning she stood outside the dungeon. Her words of courage and faith are memorable:

> Fear not, the cause is God's for which you are here, and he will plead it himself. Therefore, be not concerned for me and the children; he that feeds the young ravens will be merciful to us: he will give you strength for your day and after we have suffered awhile, he will perfect that which is lacking in our souls, and then bring us 'where the wicked cease from troubling and the weary are at rest.'

As Nelson looked at his brave wife, likely to be left alone with two children and with a third due shortly, he found fresh strength to endure his suffering, and responded, 'I cannot fear either man or devil, so long as I find the love of God as I do now.'

No justice could be expected for a despised Methodist preacher, and even though many pleaded for Nelson's release, demonstrating beyond contradiction that he was no troublemaker, their words fell on deaf ears. One man offered five hundred pounds bail for him, but it was useless. Marched first to Leeds and then on to York, Nelson lost no opportunity for exhorting bystanders wherever he could find any to listen. Reports of these events flew swiftly from town to town, and everywhere he was taken the crowds thronged the streets, either to ridicule or encourage him. At York Martha once more managed to contact her imprisoned husband and yet again encouraged him to endure steadfastly. 'We do not fear,' she maintained, 'for our God is as able to deliver now as he was seventeen hundred years ago.'

In the event the brave stonemason preacher was finally released through the intervention of the Countess of Huntingdon, several months later, but not before he had used his captivity to preach to the coarse military community and to many others who would never otherwise have heard the gospel of God's grace.

After these glimpses of a woman of staunch Christian fortitude, Martha Nelson disappears off the canvas of recorded history. But for the next thirty years she courageously supported her preacher husband, through poverty, persecution and pain. With increasing demands on his ministry, John Nelson was to cast in his lot fully with the early Methodist movement and at John Wesley's instructions would travel the length and breadth of the country. We catch sight of him as far from home as Land's End or Newcastle, Grimsby or Bristol. Frequently facing the ruthless persecution of the ignorant rabble, John Nelson was often in danger. But Martha's support never wavered, although she faced the task of bringing up a young family largely single-handed and with little finance, for itinerant preachers had no settled income at that time.

But with her husband she too would have entered into the gladness of witnessing an astounding work of the Spirit of God throughout Yorkshire and far beyond. When John Nelson died in 1774 at the age of sixty-seven, the crowds who followed his coffin to the graveside stretched for over half a mile. Leeds had never witnessed such a funeral before. Martha, who was two years his senior, outlived her brave husband by only two months. Then she joined him once more in that land of joy long anticipated, a land where cruelty and injustice are found no more.

John Blackader: Resolute Covenanter

John Blackader was one of the most notable of the Scottish Covenanters. Like their English counterparts, the later Puritans, the Covenanters suffered both eviction from their churches and intense persecution after the Restoration of Charles II to the throne in 1660. Some of the more courageous of the Covenanters became field-preachers, risking their lives to minister to the spiritual needs of the people wherever they had opportunity.

A frightened child was lying face down in the loft of his home. With one eye glued to a chink in the floorboards, he was watching with horror the scene being enacted in the room below. With bared swords soldiers were slashing through furnishings and thrusting their weapons into every conceivable hiding-place. Together with his mother, brothers and sisters, the boy had fled to the loft as brutal-looking men had burst into their home searching for his father, John Blackader. Suddenly 'a murdering ruffian,' as the child was later to describe him, glanced up and caught sight of the bright little eye gazing down at him. Without a second thought he lunged upwards with his sword, only missing the chink in the floorboards by less than an inch.

October 1662 was a dark month for the church of Jesus Christ in Scotland, comparable only to Black Bartholomew's Day in England two months earlier. Then two thousand English pastors and teachers had been evicted from their livings for their unwillingness to comply with the terms of the Act of Uniformity. Now all Scottish preachers were required to seek reordination at the hands of the bishops—a measure to which few could submit in good conscience. The Act, known as the Glasgow Act, was signed by men who, we are told, 'were all so drunk that day that they were not capable of considering anything that was laid before them.' It went on to stipulate that all those who would not comply should lose their ministries forthwith, their pulpits being declared vacant. Parishioners were to be relieved of the obligation of contributing to the support of such men, and could face heavy penalties if they continued to hear them preach. The drunken compilers of this retrograde legislation imagined that most of Scotland's preachers were like themselves, loving security and income above considerations of conscience. They anticipated that no more than ten men would prove awkward, and refuse reordination. In the event over four hundred Scottish preachers chose poverty, homelessness, suffering and even death rather than the path of compromise.

John Blackader had entered the ministry in the parish of Troqueer, near Dumfries, in 1653, when he was thirty-seven years of age. Untaught and abandoned in their way of life, his people had responded only slowly to the challenge of their new ministry. But now, nine years later, not only his regular hearers, but the whole neighbourhood, had been deeply affected through the transforming power of the gospel. All who could read were encouraged to possess their own Bibles; children were regularly taught and family worship established in the homes of his parishioners.

Blackader continued preaching throughout that October of 1662. But on the last Sunday of the month, as he was warning his people against the danger of accepting false teaching from any hireling pastor who might fill his pulpit after he had gone, news came of the approach of the king's dragoons commissioned to arrest the bold preacher who had refused to submit to the terms of the new act. His congregation wept as their pastor hurried away to find shelter in some nearby home.

Unable to track down their quarry at his church, the dragoons waited under cover until the following morning. Feeling sure that Blackader would assume they had given up the search and would therefore have returned to his home, they stormed into the manse. Convinced he was concealed somewhere, they proceeded to ransack the place. But failing to discover the preacher, the heartless dragoons turned their spite on the frightened family. Blackader's wife, his two small sons and infant daughter were roughly evicted. 'Bag and baggage we who were children were put into cadger's creels,' recalled the younger of the two boys many years later. As these large panniers were slung across the backs of horses, the children were carried off to the nearby parish of Glencairns. Distressed parishioners lined the road as the horses, laden with their human cargo, passed by.

'I'm banish't, I'm banish't,' wailed a young voice from the depths of one of the panniers.

'Who has banished you?' enquired a sympathetic onlooker.

'Bite-the-sheep has banish't me,' came the boy's disconsolate rejoinder, doubtless using a phrase he had heard in his home.

Never again would John Blackader and his family enjoy a settled life together. A marked man, he would be hunted night and day as an enemy of the state. For some time, perhaps several years, he feared to preach or venture far from his places of hiding in Galloway, knowing the cruel reprisals that would follow for himself and his family if he were caught. But the needs of the people, now cowed and dispirited without the consolations of the ministry, weighed heavily on his heart. Cautiously at first, but then with increasing boldness, John Blackader began to preach once more. And the people, well aware that they could face prohibitive fines, scourging and even branding with hot irons, if they were found listening to him, were still willing to risk all for the sake of benefiting once more from Blackader's ministry.

Together with such men as John Welsh and Gabriel Semple, he became known as a 'field-preacher.' These men would appoint a secret location where services were to be held. Quietly the information was spread from hamlet to farmstead. Then men, women and children would slip silently from their homes and gather together in many a hidden wood and glen to hear the words of life from these true shepherds of Christ's flock.

But four years after his eviction an event took place which gave John Blackader a new boldness and a courage to preach yet more widely regardless of personal cost. Strangely enough, it was renewed persecution that brought this about, and once more it was his family that bore the brunt of the suffering. Early in 1666, Sir James Turner, one of the most vitriolic perpetrators of the sufferings of the Scottish church, returned to Galloway searching for Blackader. The home where the family was living was discovered, but this time both Blackader and his wife were absent, having just set out for Edinburgh in search of safer accommodation for the family. Only a nurse and servant were in the house caring for the children, who now included a new-born baby.

Surrounding the house at about two o'clock in the morning, loud-mouthed and violent, the dragoons demanded entrance. Unable to believe that they had missed their man again, they began to smash up the furniture to make a fire. 'They stabbed through beds and bedclothes' in case he should be hiding there, and then 'threw down his books upon the floor and caused poor me to hold the candle till they had examined them,' recollected one of the boys. Still not satisfied at the mayhem they had created, the dragoons entered the loft where the family's poultry was quietly roosting. Grabbing the birds, they wrung their necks one by one until they had destroyed them all. And so they proceeded with their destructive raid, even threatening to roast the terrified children in the fire, until one distressed boy fled out into the night wearing only his nightshirt. For half a mile the ten-year-old stumbled through the darkness until he came to the next village, where he hoped he might find shelter. But every door was shut for the villagers were all asleep. Reaching at last the village cross, the boy climbed to the top step. Here he clung, and then fell fast asleep.

'O my puir bairn,' exclaimed an old woman early next morning when she discovered the lightly-clad figure, 'who are you?'

'I am Mr Blackader's son,' replied the boy, as he described the 'fearful men with red coats' who had "burnt all our house, my breether and sister and all the family.'

'O puir thing, come in and lie down in my warm bed,' said the old woman kindly. And the boy later described that bed as 'the sweetest bed I ever met with.'

When John Blackader learnt of the sufferings inflicted on his young family for his sake, he decided to move them immediately to the relative safety of Edinburgh, splitting them up at least temporarily, and placing them with friends brave enough to risk their own lives to care for them. Although this would mean that he would see far less of them, at least he had a measure of confidence regarding their security. And so, with his family in less danger, there was now nothing to prevent the bold preacher from throwing in his lot with the despised and suffering Covenanter remnant.

Ayrshire, Galloway, Fifeshire, the Lothians and the Border Counties, in all these areas Blackader could be found, consoling and ministering to the spiritual needs of the people. Each time he ventured out to preach he took his life in his hands. Who could tell whether someone in his congregation would betray him? Hiding in the woods and hamlets of Galloway, he outwitted his pursuers again and again even though there was a reward of a thousand Scottish merks offered for his arrest, alive or dead. Following some tip-off, the dragoons would swoop down with lightning speed, only to discover that Blackader was nowhere to be found. Gradually his elusiveness earned him the nickname of 'Guess-Again.'

Pressed for space on one occasion, Blackader's congregation, meeting in the Woods of Dundonald, climbed the trees until the great branches groaned under the weight of his eager hearers. And always a look-out would be posted to give early warning of any approach of the king's dragoons. For not only could the preacher suffer imprisonment and even death if he were caught, but anyone who showed him kindness or offered him shelter could face severe retribution. A moving and powerful preacher, Blackader would console his listeners by reminding them of the ultimate victory of the Son of God over all his enemies. Equally he would woo the undecided to embrace the suffering Saviour by faith to the saving of their souls.

As the political situation deteriorated and tension rose, the possibility of violent intrusion from militia men into these services of public worship steadily increased. By 1670 it was becoming customary for the look-out men to carry arms to defend both preacher and people if necessary.

In the summer of that year Blackader was to be found north of the Firth of Forth near Dunfermline. A well-documented account of a conventicle or field-meeting has survived, held in a place known as Hill o'Beath. Here the expectant people had been gathering since first light to listen to Blackader and other field-preachers, for the day's services were due to begin by eight o'clock. Taking as his text, 'For he must reign till he hath put all enemies under his feet,' Blackader again encouraged the beleaguered Covenanter remnant to renew their confidence in the power and final purposes of God. The crowd hung on every word, not knowing how long it might be before they had any further opportunities to hear their preachers again.

But during the afternoon preaching service the people began to be aware that armed infiltrators were actually present, mingling among the worshippers. A lieutenant was sitting astride his horse not far from the preacher himself. Wary and nervous, Blackader's protectors began to draw out their weapons until Blackader, becoming conscious of the disturbance, paused in the middle of his sermon. Locating the cause of the unrest, he addressed the officer directly: 'Let me see, sir, who will offer to wrong you. They shall as soon wrong myself, for we come here to do violence to no man, but to proclaim the gospel of peace. If you be pleased to stay you are as welcome as any.' Disarmed by such persuasive words, the lieutenant heard the sermon through to its conclusion and then cantered off without causing further trouble. Riding back to Edinburgh himself that night after a long day of preaching, fraught with tensions, Blackader found that the ferryman, realizing his identity, would not risk taking him across the Firth of Forth on his ferry. Blackader was obliged to ride many extra miles until he could cross the river at Stirling—a further eight hours in the saddle.

Another and even more memorable field-meeting took place later that same year as a communion service was celebrated in Dumfriesshire. In a secluded meadow by a river, with the wooded hills rising up behind, the vast congregation, estimated at over three thousand, gathered to listen to Blackader, John Welsh and other field preachers. Look-out men took up their positions on the outskirts to warn of any approaching dragoons. 'Amidst the lonely mountains we remembered the words of our Lord that true worship was not peculiar to Jerusalem or Samaria—that the beauty of holiness consisted not in material temples,' wrote Blackader. The services lasted for three days, culminating in the communion service itself—a privilege long denied to the people. Serious-faced and intent, they ate and drank the memorials of Christ's atoning sacrifice, knowing well the personal price they might have to pay. Rough stones formed the communion tables at which they sat down in orderly groups of a hundred at a time.

The service proceeded without any hostile interruptions: 'It was indeed the Lord who covered us a table in the wilderness, in presence of our foes, and reared a pillar of glory between us and the enemy, like the fiery cloud of old,' wrote Blackader. A day never to be forgotten, it was marked by an unusual sense of the presence of Christ. Our 'souls breathed in a diviner element and burned upwards as with the fire of a pure and holy devotion,' he later commented.

Not always could the government rely on its militia men to break up these vast field-gatherings, however. On one occasion in 1674 Blackader had the boldness to arrange a conventicle at Kinkell, only a mile from St Andrews—the residence of Archbishop Sharp, perpetrator of much of the suffering endured by the Covenanters. Enraged at such audacity, the archbishop ordered the militia men to disperse the gathering immediately and to arrest the preacher. To his consternation and anger he was informed that no dragoons were available for the task: all had gone to hear the preacher for themselves. That day the presence and power of God were so signally manifest among the people that many rough and hardened soldiers were seen to be weeping as they listened to Blackader's preaching. One militia man in particular, whose harsh spirit had already marked him out as a man to be feared, was so deeply moved by all he saw and heard that his tears flowed freely as he was convicted of his sinful state.

For two short periods, in 1678 and 1680, Blackader left Scottish shores for a brief respite in Rotterdam where many Covenanters had gathered—exiles of the persecution in their homeland. Relieved from the tension of constant vigilance and the ever-present fear of betrayal, Blackader was refreshed by fellowship with such men as Robert M'Ward and John Brown of Wamphray. With strengthened spirit and renewed courage, the field-preacher returned once more to his fugitive life of sacrifice and service, as he ministered to congregations bereft of their legitimate pastors.

And so for almost twenty years John Blackader travelled and preached in all weathers and under all conditions. Even deep snow could not hinder a people who hungered after the Word of God, and so they pulled up handfuls of heather to form some protection from the damp as they sat to listen. Describing these determined worshippers, Blackader's early biographer wrote, 'Denied the privilege of worshipping in temples made with hands, they made the lonely hills their pulpits, their sanctuary the high places of the field. They sought the mist and cloud to hide them from the vigilance and fury of their pursuers... To them the terror of the elements was less appalling than their inhuman oppressors, and the wildest scenery in nature wore a more friendly aspect than the face of man.'

But the fearless preacher was caught at last. On 5 April 1681 his ever-vigilant enemies were awaiting him when he paid a clandestine visit to his family in Edinburgh. Early in the morning, when only Blackader's daughter and a servant girl were up, came a soft knock at the door. Presuming it to be friends, his daughter opened the door, but her mistake soon became apparent as the town mayor entered accompanied by a troop of soldiers. Her father was ordered to dress before being escorted to the home of the ageing but ruthless General Dalyell. Blackader asked if he might speak in his own defence. 'You have spoken too much,' was the callous reply. 'I would hang you with my own hands.'

No fair trial was afforded to this upright servant of Jesus Christ as he appeared before a hastily assembled council later that day. Questions were framed in a form that would compel him to speak words designed to seal his own condemnation. Completing their inquisition the following day, the council ordered Blackader to wait in an adjoining room while they deliberated his fate. Three hours later soldiers entered the room to hustle the resolute Covenanter off to prison on the Bass Rock.

Purchased for the Crown in 1671, this storm-beaten rock in the Firth of Forth was a fortress from which none could escape. Only a third of a mile in diameter, it afforded scant protection from the elements. Waves over thirty feet high would pound against the prison walls, while the roar of wind and sea would reverberate around that lonely stronghold. The cells, described as 'dank, damp, dripping and squalid,' often made the prisoners 'envy the very birds of the air their freedom,' as one hard-pressed old Covenanter was to express it. The only consolation for John Blackader was the presence of like-minded men with whom to share both his meagre rations of dried fish and oatmeal and, more importantly, the common consolation of a refuge and a glory beyond the pain and suffering of their earthly lot.

Blackader, now well into his sixties, soon found his health deteriorating under the strict regime of foul cells and little recreation. His once powerful frame became bowed by rheumatism, and reduced by dysentery, which he contracted from being obliged to drink melted snow in winter and water from stagnant rock pools in summer. In stormy weather the prisoners often went without food altogether, for no supply boat could approach the rock in safety under such conditions.

For five years this stalwart Covenanter languished on the Bass Rock. Eventually a petition for his discharge was granted. But it was too late. Constant even in death, he was heard to declare, 'The Lord will yet arise and defend his own cause and subdue all his enemies.' And on 3 December 1685 Blackader was released at last from the biting cold of his cramped, unhealthy cell and the endless, gnawing pain into the freedom of the city of God, 'a glorious and triumphant martyr for the name of Jesus,' as one of his sons later wrote.